# IMAGES OF
# HOLINESS

# IMAGES OF HOLINESS

**Explorations in Contemporary Spirituality**

## PHILIP SHELDRAKE, S.J.

AVE MARIA PRESS   NOTRE DAME, INDIANA 46556

First published in 1987 by Darton, Longman and Todd Ltd. 89 Lillie Road, London, SW6 1UD.

© 1987 by Philip Sheldrake.

Published in the United States by Ave Maria Press.

© 1988 by Philip Sheldrake.

International Standard Book Number:  0-87793-384-7
0-87793-385-5 (pbk.)

Library of Congress Catalog Card Number: 88-71022

Cover design by Robert L. Mutchler

Printed and bound in the United States of America

# Contents

# Acknowledgements

Of the material in this book, chapters 1, 2, 3 and 7 have not been published previously. Chapter 4 is a substantial revision of a conference paper recently published in *The Way Supplement*, 58, Spring 1987. The second half of chapter 5 makes use of some material previously published in *The Way Supplement*, 48, Autumn 1983. Chapters 6 and 8 appeared respectively in *The Way Supplement*, 54, Autumn 1985, and in *The Way*, April 1984, but have been slightly revised for this book. Some of the unpublished material originated in talks, workshops or discussions conducted for the 1985 staffs' conference of Anglican theological colleges, the students of St John's College, Nottingham and the participants of the 1984–86 ecumenical training course for spiritual directors at the Institute of Spirituality, Heythrop College, London.

I am grateful to all those people who have heard or read material included in this book and whose questions and reactions were invaluable in revising or developing my ideas. I owe a particular debt of gratitude to Victoria Le Fanu at Darton, Longman and Todd for her detailed criticisms of the text. Michael Barnes SJ, David Lonsdale SJ and Lavinia Byrne IBVM read the complete manuscript at different stages of its development and their comments as well as their patience and interest were deeply appreciated. Lastly, Teresa de Bertodano of Darton, Longman and Todd has been a continuous source of encouragement and practical advice.

Most of the Scripture quotations in this book are taken from the New Jerusalem Bible published and copyright 1985 by Darton, Longman and Todd Ltd and Doubleday & Co Inc, and are used by permission of the

ACKNOWLEDGEMENTS

publishers. A few are from the Revised Standard Version
of the Bible, copyrighted 1971 and 1952 by the Division of
Christian Education of the National Council of Churches
of Christ in the USA.

# Introduction

My experience of teaching both in adult education courses and in a school of theology has made me aware of a number of problems associated with the meaning of the word 'spirituality' as well as its supposed content. Many people who are initially attracted to such courses assume that the subject will be limited to practical questions and to special 'spiritual' activities such as prayer. In giving retreats and spiritual direction over ten years or so I have also found similar problems: our relationship with God is confined to spiritual experiences in the narrow sense and does not enter effectively into the major part of daily life. Equally, there is a divide between head and heart – between the way we think about our faith and the way in which we pray or otherwise express our commitment as Christians. Finally, some of us are still imprisoned in a spirituality that is not just personal (which is a good thing) but also individualistic and find it difficult to draw together our prayer and the social or political issues of the wider world. This is something with which I have had to come to terms in my own life in recent years. In a sense, all these problems embody 'theologies' that are dualistic or in other words make a sharp distinction between the sacred and secular dimensions of our lives.

It seems to me vital that we broaden our understanding. Spirituality is not just about the heart and feelings or about practice, but must be drawn into our questioning about faith. The Christian life is not merely concerned with interiority or 'spiritual' matters but involves all the elements of our experience. We should not be concerned merely with our individual growth but with the communal and social dimensions of our existence. This wider appreciation of

spirituality is relatively recent and is, in part, a rediscovery
of a more ancient tradition. This is clear once we begin to
study the contents of journals and books on spirituality
over the last twenty years. The earlier publications concentrated almost exclusively on prayer, penance, the theological virtues and other classical themes; the most recent
works seek to address questions arising from the everyday
experience of Christians as well as the relationship between
the Christian spiritual tradition and major social or
political issues.

A friend once described spirituality to me as 'theology
on two feet'. In other words, 'spirituality' (at least in a
Christian context) is a useful term to describe how, indi-
vidually and collectively, we personally appropriate the
traditional Christian beliefs about God, humanity and the
world and express them in terms of our basic attitudes,
life-style and activity. On a personal level, spirituality is
how we stand before God in the context of our everyday
lives. For Christians this involves two complementary
dimensions: our tradition, and our experience of the culture
and world in which we live, by which we are influenced
and to which we respond. The question of how these two
dimensions relate to each other is a complex one. However,
in simple terms, we must certainly do justice to both. We
cannot exclude elements of our experience which do not
conveniently fit a simplistic or over-rigid understanding of
what is, after all, a rich and many-sided Christian
tradition. We must allow our experience to question our
grasp of the tradition – to help us to see it in new ways.
For example, in personal terms, I can see that my presuppositions about ministry in the Church were more effectively challenged by an experience of lay Christians,
including women, exercising real and effective ministry
than by abstract arguments. Equally, however, our
tradition helps us to interpret our experience, to give it
significance and meaning, and indeed is the inherited
framework within which we come to any experience
whether we are conscious of it at the time or not.

I believe that, in practice, spirituality finds its starting
point in experience rather than in abstract ideas. Histori-
cally we can see that all great movements in the Church,

or 'schools' of spirituality, arose in response to specific needs and circumstances and have roots in particular cultures and eras whose perspectives they initially reflected. Christians of every age and culture, therefore, have to be aware of the signs of their time and place and to interpret the Gospel of Jesus anew.

In my own attempts to reflect personally on spirituality over the last few years I had to begin by trying to analyse some, at least, of the questions and problems that contemporary life poses, and it is to this attempt that I turn my attention in the first chapter. I feel that this has a particular urgency in our times because Christianity and the world in which it exists seems to me to be at a crossroads, a point of crisis. Someone suggested to me recently that, while change is in some ways continuous, we have reached a particularly crucial break-point in history similar to the effects that the Renaissance, Reformation or Industrial Revolution had on Western consciousness. Traditional institutions – social, political, economic and religious – are under pressure because, while created in one world, they are straining to deal with a situation that is, like it or not, impervious to the answers of the past and which presents an apparently overwhelming number of new questions.

This book falls into two sections: on the Christian life and on prayer. I do not pretend that what I have to say is particularly systematic or comprehensive. What I have written is the result of my own experience as well as some years of teaching, retreats and spiritual counselling and reflects a selection of some of the important issues that have arisen for me and for the people I have attempted to accompany. I have tried as best I can to rethink the tradition on central elements of the Christian life in the light of some of the issues and questions that have arisen from my attempts to reflect upon the contemporary context for spirituality. But each of us must attempt to read the signs of the times for ourselves and to reinterpret our understanding of such things as holiness and prayer as a consequence.

I begin with our understanding of the Christian life in general because it seems to me that any discussion of prayer must have as its context the way we try as a whole to respond to the call of Christ. Because this life has been, and still is, understood in terms of a search for holiness and because the element of struggle is both so central and at the same time ambiguous it seems reasonable to begin here. A renewed emphasis on theologies of the Cross is, in different ways, refocusing our attention on the notion of unconditioned 'discipleship' in the footsteps of Jesus suffering and poor as a crucial framework for understanding the Christian life – not least holiness and asceticism. I therefore end the section with some reflections on the implications of this for contemporary spirituality.

All questions about the nature and practice of prayer relate to the 'God question' and so I felt it was important to reflect on some of the images of God that we have and their roots both in theology and experience as well as their practical implications. For example how does our image of God affect what we think prayer is? Much of the material here originates in retreats with which I have been involved or in discussion groups where the subject has been reflected upon and not simply in more technical classes to students. This led my reflections quite naturally to the specific ways we understand the practice of prayer – and particularly to the fact that much writing on the subject, even today, assumes that the ideal model is structured, formal periods of time. This partly reflects our understanding of what prayer is which itself is based on our images of God. However it is also in the light of the concrete difficulties experienced by people whom I have tried to accompany and of the feelings of inadequacy that often result that I felt it important to show that the Christian tradition on prayer is much wider than many of us imagine.

Our images of God and of prayer clearly affect the way in which we manage or fail to make the connection between prayer and life in general, or prayer and social awareness in particular and it is to this issue that I turn next. It is becoming more and more apparent that the two contemporary Christian preoccupations with contemplation and justice must be brought together, precisely because without the other each is likely to fail in its purpose. The search for God at the heart of specifically Christian prayer is also a search for the divine presence in all aspects of human life. The search for the justice of the Kingdom needs a contemplative dimension if it is not to become merely another ideology that can dehumanise us. I decided to end with a reflection on the way of praying known as gospel contemplation or 'prayer of the imagination' because it has been so badly misunderstood in the past, and because, in the lives of many contemporary Christians, it is proving such a potent instrument not only of self-discovery but also of a broader consciousness of the world.

While I hope that what I write has a measure of coherence it is no more than a reflection on some of the issues that seem to me to lie at the heart of many contemporary Christians' search for holiness, wholeness and the fullness of discipleship. There are, I feel, a number of unifying factors. Firstly, while I hope that they show an awareness of the riches of our inherited tradition, the chapters attempt to rethink it in the light of contemporary questions. Secondly, the writing is not purely devotional or practical but tries to provide the beginnings of a theoretical and in particular a theological framework, in non-technical language as far as possible, for thinking about spirituality and prayer. Thirdly, at all points, I have attempted to do justice to the need for a social spirituality and particularly for a link between discipleship and social compassion. Finally, it would be strange if my own spiritual tradition, the Ignatian one, had not coloured what I have written. This is implicit at most points but because of much misunderstanding in the past as well as because of the current increase of interest in Ignatian spirituality, not only in my own Communion but beyond, it seemed useful to attempt to go into a little more detail where that seemed particularly helpful.

Much of what I have learned from other people over the years has been absorbed, consciously or otherwise, into my own blood-stream and become part of my own experience. My own religious background is Roman Catholic, albeit touched from an early age by relatives and friends from other Churches. For twenty odd years I have been a member of a religious order, the Jesuits, and for ten of these I have been a priest. In itself this could have been, for all its riches, a very limiting experience. My contacts, work and friendship with Christians from several traditions, not to mention with others who would describe themselves simply as 'honest searchers', and a brief period living out of my own culture in India, have therefore been vitally important in challenging me and broadening my vision. My inherited understanding of the Christian life, the Church and ministry have had to be reassessed in the light of the experience of others. Change and growth undoubtedly continue. I am immensely grateful for this. I hope, as a result, that what follows may find an echo in Christians of different traditions and with different life-experiences who seek somehow to hold all things together in one as well as in some 'honest searchers', and that it will not be too parochial or narrowly Roman Catholic.

# 1
# The Challenge to Spirituality

When, as Christians, we ask what are the crucial questions that our age addresses to spirituality, our reflections will need to be both individual and communal. In what areas of my life am I being challenged personally to conversion and to change? How can I pray? Who is my neighbour? Collectively, what kind of Church-community are we asked to become? What kind of Christian mission are we being asked to undertake? My attempt here to reflect briefly on some of the challenges facing contemporary spirituality is necessarily very superficial. However, in the world of the late twentieth century there seem to be several important and identifiable general factors which have undermined the world view which we have inherited from the past and on which much traditional spirituality has been based.

In the first place our understanding of the cosmos has changed substantially. Our world and humankind can no longer be seen as the absolute centre of the universe. Secondly, evolutionary theory of one kind or another is accepted without question (except by certain fundamentalist Christian groups) and so the evolution of humankind is seen to be merely one of life's processes neither separate from, nor superior to the others. Thirdly, the late nineteenth and twentieth centuries have seen the acceptance of psychology as a respectable science. The consequent discovery of a vast and complex inner human world has called into question the total objectivity of human values. Finally, the social sciences, economic and political theory have questioned traditional conceptions of human society. One might add, too, that the previous optimistic and over-confident view of human progress has also been undermined more recently by the Holocaust of the Nazi era, the increasing nuclear threat and the acute hunger and poverty of much of the world which is brought to our attention daily in the media.

The previous certainties and self-reliance of Christianity have worn pretty thin in the face of the increasing challenge both of social change and the consequent uncertainties of living, and of the advances of human knowledge which to a considerable degree have entered into popular consciousness. Any contemporary attempt, therefore, to construct a viable spirituality must take into consideration the new world view of science with which religion has to dialogue. Equally, a fuller understanding of human life, represented especially perhaps by psychology, makes the former assumption of a body/soul, material/spiritual dichotomy untenable. In other words, spirituality will no longer be concerned merely with the 'soul' but with the whole person, and its attitude to the body and to material things in general will not be one of rejection. A renewed understanding of the essentially social nature of human existence, the interdependence of different societies and the effect on all of us of social and economic structures will mean that spirituality will increasingly do justice to the social context for religious consciousness. The relationship between personal spirituality and the shaping of future human society and the responsibility of Christians for building a world of justice and peace are increasing concerns. Finally, inter-denominational ecumenism and inter-faith dialogue mean that people are increasingly prepared to look beyond their immediate religious culture for assistance in their search for a way to God. Equally ecumenism forces us to look at our inherited traditions in a new and questioning way. I would now like to explore a little further some of these elements because I believe that they are particularly crucial for any of us who are concerned to reflect about contemporary spirituality.

*Spirituality and theology*

I strongly believe that there can be no true theology without spirituality and vice versa. In theological circles, however, spirituality still suffers from a tarnished reputation born of centuries of distinguishing the intellectual from the 'feeling' dimension of religion. At the risk of being over-simplistic one can say that in the New Testament doctrine is seen as life and that 'theology' is therefore always 'spiritual'. In St Paul's 'spiritual person' (1 Cor 2: 13–15; 9:11; 14:1 for example) there is a harmonious unity between belief and life. Christian writers in the early centuries of the Church followed the same lines. Theology was not just intellectual activity; it was also love insepar- able from prayer (for example 'wisdom' as understood in St Augustine, or 'loving contemplation' in St Gregory). This unity between the mind and heart reached its supreme expression in the West in the age of the monastic theology of Anselm and Bernard of Clairvaux. It is really only with Peter Abelard that theology began to mean intellectual speculation alone and the beginning of what came to be called scholasticism or 'the theology of the schools'. However, the very greatest of the 'scholastic' theologians such as Thomas Aquinas and Bonaventure continued to maintain a unity between intellectual reflection and contemplation.

Only in late scholasticism, as what we call the Middle Ages drew to a close, did the chasm widen between intellect and will and a fundamental split appear. Two theologies developed: one theoretical and 'scientific', the other devotional and affective and increasingly unrelated to solid doctrine. Thus the academic theologian became a specialist in an independent area of knowledge and the devout Chris- tian was offered next to nothing theologically to clarify his or her life and prayer. Spirituality, as a consequence, became increasingly subjective and individualistic. Its basic concern was with private consent to God. Personal faith was put beyond discussion and isolated from intellec- tual questioning. Experience easily became an end in itself. Later, with the advent of the Enlightenment in the late seventeenth and eighteenth centuries, there was a growth of scientific enquiry as a way to certainty. The result was what has been termed a 'dissociation of sensibility' that severed the connections between thought and feeling, mind and heart.

To theologians, spirituality became an object of

suspicion. It was seen as unrealistic because associated with theologically dubious devotion, optional because it belonged only to a certain cast of mind or temperament. Because spirituality seemed preoccupied with inwardness and introspection it was felt to be detached from its culture and age and indifferent to history. The divorce between theology and spirituality was a misfortune for both. Theology became increasingly remote and theoretical and spirituality increasingly subjective and self-authenticating because not amenable to serious questioning. To be fair, this situation has changed a great deal in recent decades. There is now a much greater awareness of the importance of bridging the gap between spirituality and serious theology, of recognising that all spirituality incarnates, at least implicitly, a definite theology or set of beliefs about God, the world and humankind. Equally theology or any structure of belief necessarily involves expression and has implications for our Christian life-style.

A student of theology needs to be a contemplative as well. Just as a contemplative attitude is prior to any fruitful Christian action as opposed to unreflective and restless activity that lacks true direction, so the process of reflecting on belief involves an honest and personal openness to the object of study. Without the marriage of spirituality with theological reflection, we lack the means to appropriate personally that reflection. If we underrate spirituality we risk the exclusion of affectivity from faith, turning doctrine into presuppositions untouched by experience and thus perpetuating a false division between head and heart, objective doctrines and personal faith. If, on the other hand, we underrate the theological roots of spirituality we risk subjectivism and the loss of criteria for judging or discerning our personal religious experience. The intensity of feelings or the brightness of an intuition is no guarantee of divine origin or truthfulness! As a student of theology I had to struggle to bring the two parts of my experience together. Perhaps it was a good thing not to be spoon-fed, and in any case the marriage of head and heart is a very personal thing. However, we received very little indication that such a task was important. It does not surprise me that, as a result, some students of theology suffer from a kind of schizophrenia, with a critical theology in one compartment and uncritical piety, or conservative devotion, in another.

The roots of Christian spirituality lie in seeking to answer the question, 'What kind of God do we have?' To talk about a Trinitarian God, Christ as God Incarnate, or the indwelling Spirit are not merely fine academic points but statements with practical implications. We live what we affirm. Not a few writers have pointed out that inadequate theologies of God inevitably result in ineffective and disembodied spiritualities. In this sense, the quality of a resulting spirituality is an important test of the adequacy of the theology that it expresses. It is not unfair to suggest that a contemporary resurgence of theories about God that in different ways undermine the reality of the Incarnation, that God truly became one of us in Jesus, in fact upsets that delicate balance of the transcendence-immanence of God which governs the way we understand and respond to life and the world.

The continual task, therefore, of theology is to draw our spirituality back to its sources in the Christian tradition about God encapsulated in the doctrines of Trinity and Incarnation. However certain contemporary explorations in theology challenge our understanding of the Christian life and prayer in a particular way. The re-emergence of rich theologies of the Cross (not least as an important element of liberation theology) is, as I shall suggest later, the basis for important changes in perspective about the nature of discipleship. The Christian tradition has, of course, always implicitly understood that God transcends our distinctions of gender and therefore our common tendency to use exclusively male language. In practice, however, the feminine aspect of God has received little explicit theological attention until recently. The 'crisis' for our inherited understanding of God produced by the feminist critique, and which goes far deeper merely than questions of language, has important consequences for the spirituality of all Christians and not only women.

*A spirituality of catholicity*

The sense of discontinuity and disintegration, cultural and religious, current among many of us in the West apparently contrasts starkly with the basic Christian affirmation that all things finally hold together in one. Ultimately structures cannot 'hold together in one', for they necessarily change and are, at all times, diverse. Rather the deepest principle of unity is the inward continuity of prayer and our shared Christian experience. At the very heart of the Christian tradition is the prayer of Eucharist which links together past and present and future in *anamnesis* – the 'memory' of God and what God has done. Here the world of time and particular places is brought in touch with eternity. So prayer and contemplation must return to the centre of Christian life instead of being treated as, at best, of secondary importance and, at worst, as irrelevant. The basic question raised by the contemplative tradition is the very nature of time and space. The contemporary loss of a sense of continuity and tradition leads us to be imprisoned increasingly in the assumptions of our particular era. Space and time are contracted to the 'here and now'. But in contemplative 'concentration' they can expand into the whole universe. In Christ is all time, all places and all experience.

We need, it seems to me, to recover a real sense of 'catholicity', of what 'holding together in one' truly means. Catholicity points to an openness that is capable of discovering and responding to reflections of what is deepest and most important in my own experience and tradition as they appear in traditions and expressions that initially I find alien. Not so long ago a friend said to me that he felt that the 'Protestant mentality' and the 'Catholic mentality' were fundamentally incompatible. Viewed in sectarian terms, where 'Protestant' and 'Catholic' describe two complete, alternative and self-contained world-views, this makes sense. However 'catholicity' is not a sectarian concept but rather an invitation for us to grow in an attitude of inclusiveness to the degree that is compatible with our integrity as Christians. To be 'catholic' is always to know that what I now am and have is not complete, needs to be completed, enriched, broadened. To be 'catholic' is to be able to be challenged to accept the gift of what I do not already possess – indeed to know that I do not possess everything. For me, one of the strongest experiences of not being complete and at the same time of being enriched came during a year in India where, for the first time in my life, I found myself in a small minority culturally and religiously. It was a profoundly disturbing experience and yet, at the same time, a period of real growth humanly and spiritually as all my unquestioned assumptions came in for serious challenge.

Catholicity undermines exclusivity, the idolatry of possession and possessiveness in my religion. 'We have, you have not.' 'You cannot possibly have because you are not one of us.' There is an arrogance, a condescension and a smugness in our labels for ourselves and for others. We talk as if we *are* Catholic, *are* Reformed, *are* Evangelical. None of us *is* truly these things. All are called to become them. A truly 'catholic' Christianity cannot by definition adopt a sectarian mentality. Personally I have found great riches in the writings of the seventeenth-century Anglican poet and parish priest, George Herbert, even allowing for his elements of Calvinism rather than by 'screening them out'. Seventeenth-century Anglican divines, not to mention many contemporary Anglican and Methodist friends (and not merely of the 'Catholic' tradition) have found much fruit in the spirituality of such 'Counter-Reformation' spiritual writers as Ignatius Loyola or Francis de Sales. Our own spirituality is immeasurably deepened by the absorption of insights from traditions that are not our own. Our catholicity is broadened. We are called from our sectarian corners to welcome a healthy plurality of Christian expressions and experiences. More and more we find ourselves reflecting in our own experience the sense that Thomas Merton had that he was called to unite in himself the thought and devotion of East and West and in that to prepare for the reunion of divided Christendom.

Our catholicity must also be a cultural one. So much traditional spirituality has reflected a narrowly European way of seeing things. If we take the experiential roots of spirituality seriously we must accept that the particular social and cultural experiences of, for example, Africa and Asia will give rise to new forms of Christian expression. While these, like all spiritualities, are particular to a time and a place, there will also be elements that eventually may transcend the local and show signs of universalism. In any case, the spiritualities of cultures other than the European must be taken seriously on their own terms in a Church that claims to be truly catholic. Equally, without being naive in our identification of common features, a truly catholic Christian spirituality will be open to the spiritual paths of the other great world faiths. This openness, to be valid, should not ignore the specific cultural and social roots of non-Christian ways of understanding religious experience. Openness, dialogue and learning from each other is not a question of seeking to create a 'generic' spirituality that artificially transcends the boundaries of particular cultures and religious structures.

Catholicity does not therefore mean believing that all religious beliefs, traditions or structures are entirely relative or as good as each other nor divorcing contemplation from faith and beliefs. All of us, too, have to grapple with what it might mean to affirm that the Body of Christ is essentially united in faith while it is, at the same time, externally fragmented. That is why contemplation is such a vital activity, for it is there where time and eternity, the particular and the universal intersect that we can recognise this God-given oneness as a prelude to recovering visible unity. Contemplation offers the possibility of a wholeness of vision that means that we need no longer be cut off from large parts of our collective Christian inheritance but rather have access to all.

To become 'Catholic' means to change as a matter of course, as a way of life. We have to learn how to let go, to have our idols regularly shattered. Coping with change is perhaps one of the greatest problems within the Church. Does my spirituality provoke me to change or is it a safe cocoon, a haven 'out of the swing of the sea', a reinforcement of certainties that leaves me where I am? Even if we accept change, how do we view it? Do we see it as occasional, exceptional, or cataclysmic – long periods of immobility followed by a sudden rush forward? Or do we understand (and this is where a sense of history is crucial) that change is continual? Put another way, do we see that change is part of what we mean by our credal definition of the Church as 'Catholic' – as continaully in search of catholicity? Do we really take to heart the image of the Church as a living 'Body' where change means life and lack of it means slow decay and ultimately death? In other words, do we see the Church as a 'thing' or as a living organism?

How we understand the role of God's Spirit (that is, theologically, the kind of pneumatology we have) is particularly relevant here. We can see the Spirit essentially as preserver, as keeping the truth, or keeping us on that straight and narrow way that not only leads us to life but which is predetermined and defined. The role of the Spirit is to preserve a 'perfect' Church which is already known in its fullness, fully in possession of itself and fully conscious of its necessary way of being. On the contrary, I would maintain that the Spirit is rather the guarantee of change, growth and development in a Church that is to be seen as an organism, on pilgrimage and ever seeking the perfection (the 'catholicity') to which it is called. The Spirit is also the one who provokes change and growth, who stimulates and challenges us out of our safe and secure ruts.

One of the greatest weaknesses in the Church is institutionalism which is the arch-enemy of catholicity. Too much religion is a bad thing – to see the Church as an end in itself is a kind of idolatry. If you see the Buddha on the road, kill him! If you see religion rearing its ugly head . . . And in 'religion' we might include: appropriate attitudes, preservation at all costs, keeping clean and tidy, rigid rules of life and structures, a certain comfort with the unacknowledged power and possessions that institutions gather around themselves.

Although there is obviously much more that could be said, I would suggest that a final aspect of 'catholicity' is the recognition of the call of all the baptised to holiness and ministry. We need to declericalise the way we understand the Church, declericalise ministry and also declericalise spirituality. The latter means developing a genuine spirituality of worldliness (which alone can form the basis for understanding the 'secular' call to holiness, and ministry from within the world). Catholicity implies an inclusive rather than an exclusive approach to God's presence, and action from within and not outside the human condition.

## A spirituality of social compassion

It is becoming increasingly clear that the problem of social justice is one of the most significant issues within particular societies and between societies: East and West, North and South. Two-thirds of the world's population do not have sufficient food, medicine or work. Most of the world has no power over either political or economic forces that control its destiny, spiritually as well as materially. A deadly arms race and, even more, the sense that such is the normal process of human relations is simply immoral – not merely because of the economic waste but because the rejection of violence is inherent to the Gospel. While no doubt rooted in the failings of individuals and groups of people, sin can in some way be seen as present in structures that maintain social or economic immorality. We cannot afford to be naive about any kind of human division and say that it is possible to live a Christian life without concern for these things. Inequality and injustice can no longer be seen merely as our natural fate. They must be understood as the effects of human selfishness. For this reason no contemporary spirituality can be effective without being rooted in social compassion.

A spirituality that is truly incarnational and includes a Gospel-centred call to be with Christ in preaching and spreading the Kingdom of God surely involves an explicitly social dimension. It is not merely a question of reforming enough individuals because individual virtue without a social conscience may not have any effect on issues of group injustice. As Christians we are called not merely to be a community ourselves but to preach and offer community to the world. Community does not, cannot exist despite or alongside injustice and human inequality. For these things dehumanise those to whom we preach love and community. The Gospel cannot be fully received in such circumstances. Working for justice is in a very real sense a condition of success in our preaching the Kingdom of God. For injustice denies the presence of God in the other and is thus a form of practical atheism. And it dehumanises us too as we, through inertia, are accomplices in the maintenance of structures of injustice and inequality. Calls for a corporate spirituality point to a need to liberate the world from all that inhibits the growth of the gospel seed. And, like it or not, this has political and economic implications because no dimension of human existence is totally autonomous – separate from the growing Kingdom of God, from the working of the Spirit. If we say that the primary Christian task is to preach the Kingdom of God, it is also the case that the promotion of justice is an essential condition of this preaching, because reconciliation with our fellow human beings follows from reconciliation with God. There can be no genuine return to the love of God unless it also involves the love of people and therefore a response to the demands of justice. To introduce people to the love of the Father means, inseparably, through him to bring them back to love of neighbour. To say otherwise is to return to a dualism that is contrary to the fundamental Christian insights about an incarnate God. A spirituality that is truly concerned with peace must necessarily be based on a realistic assessment of the world, and not merely of individuals, as in need of healing.

It is really inaccurate to talk of 'social spirituality' as if this were one kind of spirituality among many. Christian spirituality as such is social as its very roots – reflecting the society of equal relationships that is God (and which we call 'Trinity') and the irrevocable commitment of that God to our world in Christ. In other words a social spirituality is a theological and not merely a sociological issue. But if we are to say that spirituality cut off from social compassion is pure escapism and self-indulgent, it is equally clear that social or political movements that seek the eradication of injustice and inequality without a spiritual vision are in danger of becoming inhuman and even totalitarian. Without contemplative awareness it is all too easy to sacrifice people for systems, structures and theories. We substitute another, perhaps more subtle, kind of oppression and therefore sin. Jesus Christ and his work of reconciliation is the source of true justice, for it is Jesus Christ who opens the way to the complete and final freedom that we want so badly. It is important that Christians and Christian spirituality show to those who work for peace and justice without explicit religious commitment that faith is not the 'opium of the people' but rather a commitment to change the world and to make it a present sign of the 'new heaven and new earth'. Equally we can show that it is not ultimately sufficient to work for justice and peace on the organisational level alone. Behind structures and organisations there are human attitudes and tendencies which are the sources of oppression and must be eradicated.

A spirituality of social compassion necessarily draws us into confrontation with the major issues of our day: social division, economic colonialism and exploitation, international conflict and the oppression of minorities. It will also lead us to question the new materialism, the intimate connection between possessions and power that is at the heart of consumerism. In this context several contemporary thinkers have suggested that frugality and simplicity are the Christian virtues for the end of the twentieth century. None of us can ignore the rapid advance of technology and the way that it is already beginning to affect the domestic and work life of many people. The issue of technology is linked to that of justice, for its expansion (like the rapidity of the nineteenth-century Industrial Revolution) is not necessarily matched by similar advances in ethical or theological reflection. Technological advance that is not reflected upon could simply become an end in itself and thus a more sophisticated and efficient method of oppression and manipulation.

Part of our problem with coming to terms with these issues (and perhaps our discomfort with talk of a social spirituality) is that religion has become progressively privatised. Culture is no longer the theatre of God's action but merely the material for human enjoyment. Few people these days would be able to say that their deepest and most human experiences are religious or spiritual. Religion has been largely institutionalised and reactions to this have more often than not been 'fringy' or bizarre. Culture has become therapeutic as has much of the search for spiritual experiences. Our therapeutic culture does not so much offer a rival commitment to faith as the freedom from any commitment. In the face of such issues spirituality must not be merely a reflection of society and culture but also be critical. The worst kinds of spirituality are either culturally conformist or on the other hand world-rejecting. To be critical means to be neither.

## Discipleship and prayer

If, as I have suggested, spirituality necessarily reflects specific circumstances and culture and is a response to concrete realities, then it is clear that our ways of understanding Christian discipleship must change and develop in the light of some of the factors I have attempted to isolate. Our inherited ideas about a central issue such as the nature of holiness, for example, do not necessarily reflect the full richness of our Christian tradition nor are they necessarily in harmony with contemporary insights about the world and human relationships. In my attempts now to reflect on different aspects of discipleship and of prayer I trust that I remain faithful to my plea for a spirituality that is truly 'catholic' and that seeks to 'hold all things together in one'. Certainly the intimate relationship between spirituality and theology will be an implicit concern at all times. Finally, in all that I have to say, I shall attempt faithfully to move away from excessive 'interiority' and from individualism towards a spirituality that does greater justice to the collective dimension of Christian living and to the demands of social compassion.

# 2
# A Humane Holiness

Because the idea of holiness has always played such a central role in the lives of Christians, it seems important to begin with it in any attempt to reflect upon contemporary discipleship. Since the Dogmatic Constitution on the Church (*Lumen Gentium*) of Vatican II, Roman Catholics have become much more familiar with the notion of a 'universal call to holiness' based on baptismal identification with Jesus Christ. This has replaced a more elitist model where holiness was, implicitly at least, the preserve of special categories of Christians who were called to 'higher' forms of Christian life such as ordained priesthood or religious vows. While other Western Churches have not in theory suffered to the same extent from this kind of spiritual elitism, I detect nonetheless that in practice 'holiness' has been seen as the preserve of the few. Equally the insights of psychology as applied to faith have made all of us more aware of faith as a process, rather than as a static 'thing' given once for all at baptism or adult conversion, and fundamentally the same for every Christian. These two factors raise a number of questions. Is holiness the same thing for everyone? Is holiness quantifiable or observable in terms of external actions? What does growth in holiness presuppose in terms of attitudes to ordinary life?

In recent years there have been a number of historical studies of holiness from what might be called a sociological standpoint. One of the main concerns of such works has been to learn more about the values of particular societies from a study of how they view saints and sanctity. Conversely such studies suggest that understandings of holiness mirror social values and are not completely autonomous categories of experience.[1] For example, an examin-

ation of medieval saints reveals that many of them reflect
the values of the 'establishment', whether secular or ecclesi-
astical, and that such saints were used to sanction certain
ideals, or reforms or the respectablity of particular religious
communities. The recognition of the sanctity of one of its
members could also enhance the reputation of a particular
city or municipality.

Apart from 'establishment' saints, however, there were
in the Middle Ages many 'popular' saints some of whom
were never canonised nor had their popular cultus
confirmed by the official Church. Medieval popular saints
seem to manifest two characteristic impulses of general
piety: the search for moral purity and for the love of God.
Saints were seen as those people who had transcended the
normal sinfulness of human existence and who had reached
a level of relationship with God that was beyond the
commonplace. In other words, saints tended both to reflect
the aspirations of ordinary piety and to stand as a reproach
to the *de facto* materialistic values of society at large. Thus,
even if saints are, by definition, atypical, they do reflect
the values and virtues of a society even if these are normally
honoured only in the breach! Thus, for example, St Francis
of Assisi's choice of radical poverty involves a rejection of
what were seen as the characteristic sins of his time, class
and culture.

It is not surprising that the understanding of sanctity in a
particular age and culture tends to reflect the predominant
perception of sinfulness. In the medieval view of holiness,
resistance to fleshly temptations played a central role. The
fact that St Bridget of Sweden's daughter (also venerated
as a saint) was believed to have refused to breast-feed after
her mother had had sexual relations is very revealing!
Popular views of asceticism were also reinforced in a
similar way. Thus, with apologies once again to breast-
feeding, certain medieval child saints revealed a precocious
understanding of the liturgical calendar by reportedly
fasting from one breast on Ember Days in Lent.

In some ages and cultures, miracles were particularly
fascinating. Most of those recorded in medieval *vitae* were
'socially useful' and were associated with an important
aspect of popular sanctity – good works and concern for

the poor and sick. Some, however, were a mixture of straightforward fascination with extraordinary power and of affirmation of official or institutional piety. There was, for example, the saint who, about to carve a chicken for dinner, realised that it was Friday and after making the sign of the Cross and restoring the bird's feathers invited it to fly away.

In a contemporary context, some Latin American writers reflect the social and religious values of their own age and culture in their descriptions of holiness. They write of the need for 'political saints'. Many such writers would point to the late Archbishop Romero as an example of someone whose 'political' holiness came about largely within the context of conversion to the poor.[2]

If we need to realise that perceptions of holiness reflect social and cultural values, it is also important to decide whether we think that holiness is a 'state' or a process. One famous British psychotherapist, Irene Bloomfield, while basically very sympathetic to religion is also critical of much traditional thinking about spirituality (not least because she has worked a great deal with clergy and religious in distress). Too often, she claims, religion begins with a fixed ideal (a static view of holiness, for example) while therapy always begins with the individual's concrete situation.[3] I want to return to possible contrasts between a religious idea of holiness and psychology's view of wholeness later.

At this point I would simply underline that, from a religious (as well as a psychological) standpoint, I believe that the most dangerous spirituality is that of possession – being in a 'state of perfection' or even conceiving of perfection as a state at all. The moment that we feel that we have arrived, are complete, or indeed that there is a potential moment when such will be the case (when we will change from movement to mere maintenance) we are furthest from God. Holiness, as I will suggest later, has a great deal to do with a realisation and acceptance of imperfection and even failure and of the need for continual conversion. Holiness is a process, a continual movement towards God. In the end the core of the process is a realisation of all as gift which means that holiness cannot be identified simply with the performance of externals – holy actions or spiritual exercises to be fulfilled.

I would also suggest that we must ask ourselves such questions as: Who are holy people? What do we mean when we claim that X or Y is a holy person? Too often, I suspect, our ideals have been far removed from normal life. Indeed there has always been a tendency to want to smooth out the rough edges of people thought of as holy – one might also add, of things, activities and institutions thought of as holy. The traditional genre of 'Lives of the Saints' on which I was brought up frequently eliminated weakness (or reduced it to amiable eccentricity) and sought a picture of consistency for its subject. Mythology and exaggeration are also common dangers in our perceptions of holiness. To say 'He is a holy man . . .' may be tantamount to saying 'Don't you dare criticise such a person'. While cynical in the extreme, the definition of a saint in the nineteenth-century *Devil's Dictionary* contains more than a grain of truth: 'a sinner, revised and edited'. So often our understanding of holiness is a very revised and edited version of normal life.

I would now like to focus on three sets of apparently opposing ideas as a useful way of posing fundamental questions about the way we see holiness: conformity or personal call; sacred action or secular involvement; holiness or wholeness.

### Conformity or personal call

Avery Dulles in his book *Models of the Church* has some helpful comments to make concerning the way that particular models of the Church affect our understanding of holiness.[4] Amongst the most interesting things he has to say are those concerning what he calls the 'Institutional Model'. From the fifteenth to the beginning of the twentieth centuries this was the prodominant model of the Church in Roman Catholic circles. It was characterised by an emphasis on the Church as a visible society in which holiness (one of the four 'notes' of the Church in the Creed) was visible holiness rather than, primarily, interior union with God. Therefore there was a concern for the 'sanctity of means', especially those not possessed by people outside the Church (or at least assumed not to be): the sacrifice of the Mass, a full sacramental system, religious vows and the celibacy of the clergy. Not surprisingly, Roman Catholics often found it hard to accept holiness outside their community in other Churches. For example, Catholic writing tended to pass over in silence the, to present-day observers, patent sanctity of several seventeenth-century Anglican writers. If such sanctity was accepted it could only be due to the wonderful and mysterious providence of God working in individuals despite and not through the worship and life of their Churches. Meanwhile, the Catholic Church manifested its own undoubted holiness by developing forms of piety that were showy and external. Catholics tended, too frequently, to count their good works and to 'practise their piety before men'.

One of the models of the Church which gradually found more favour in this century was the 'sacramental' one. The Church was the primary sacrament. This model certainly provided some helpful correctives to the 'institutional' view of holiness just described. The Church on earth was never absolutely holy and so there was a strong emphasis on conversion and repentance – *Ecclesia semper reformanda*. Penitence was an essential aspect of a pilgrim Church and the very consciousness that its members were not worthy of their high calling was itself a testimony to holiness. There were dangers however, for the sacramental model of the Church sometimes included an excessively 'high' view of priesthood – the priest's holiness (presented primarily as separateness) was understood as, in a special way, pointing to the essential 'other-worldliness' and future orientation of the Christian life. In other words, the priest was described as an 'eschatological sign' to more ordinary mortals. This overflowed, too, into theories of the religious life. The danger was that priests and members of religious orders were set apart from the remainder of the community and surrounded by an aura of cultic holiness. Even now, the 'official' model of priesthood and religious life tends to stress living apart, a distinctive garb, special duties (such as Divine Office) and celibacy. While the latter, for clergy, is primarily the preserve of Western Catholicism, it has been said to me by Anglicans that cultic holiness is also implicit in the Church of England's (and especially Queen Elizabeth I's) original model of priesthood which was essentially celibate while allowing the concession of marriage! Certainly this is borne out by the comments of George Herbert (the seventeenth-century Anglican priest and poet) in his description of the ideals of the clerical life, *The Country Parson*.

A third model of the Church which has found much favour in recent years is the 'community' model. This puts its emphasis more on holiness as a quality of a living community. It is, therefore, described in more vitalistic and dynamic categories. It is not so closely associated with means nor is it externally and statistically measurable. It is primarily the lived holiness of interior communion with God pouring over into communion with our neighbour.

The more institutional our ideal of holiness and the more external and visible it is, the more such holiness demands conformity. The face of the Church should not be marred by conflict or eccentricity. Frequently the ideal of holiness presented is extrinsic – that is, associated with objective, abstract, or even imposed norms, and with 'appropriate' attitudes and behaviour. Those seeking a more intrinsic holiness, that is to say one that does justice to their own growth, gifts and unique relationship with God, are likely to find that their attitudes and values conflict with the accepted norm. The problem is that of rubbing up, uncomfortably, against the expectations of the community. The question obviously arises as to how important the community dimension of Christian life should be in relationship to the personal journey of faith. A reasonable community dimension to holiness, it seems to me, will in fact take seriously the uniqueness of the individual and will conceive of communal holiness less in terms of abstract norms than in terms of a proper dialogue between different emphases and between people who have personal journeys to pursue and yet appreciate the necessary community dimension of their search. An over-institutional model of holiness will demand conformity and will thereby tend to provoke a contrary reaction towards the unhealthily eccentric and excessively free-wheeling.

*Sacred action or secular involvement*

Another tension is the relationship or opposition between other-worldly and this-worldly spiritualities. Is the search for God a matter of flight or engagement? One of the most antithetical expressions of this tension is the conflict between what are seen as life-affirming and life-denying values. What do the popular perceptions of holiness actually express concerning our attitude to life itself and the value of the human? How often have we been told that 'X is a very holy person' and had profound doubts about their humanity? How far is joylessness or a pleasure-denying attitude ('You know, he never spends a penny on himself' or 'It's years since I had time to read a book or watch TV') part of the perception? Consider this paradox: the nun who is told severely by a member of her community that the fact that she tends not to wear blue, black or grey clothes means that she is 'breaking the vow of poverty'. Is it poverty that is the issue (despite the fact that she has few clothes and those inexpensive, and that the old habit now costs a fortune to make) or is it that what she wears reflects a very different and perhaps a more affirmative attitude to life?

The reduction of holiness to special activities – often, humanly speaking, odd and eccentric ones – denies the reality that the whole of life is a context for holiness. It also helps to perpetuate the idea that holiness is an elitist call open only to those who can and will live a visibly 'marginal' life. The trouble too is that such a view of holiness tends to undermine any effective witness because prophecy and challenge to the world are reduced to sideline oddity.

The increasing interest in some contemporary cults and meditation techniques means that we are sometimes faced with a revival of holiness as a kind of gnosticism – special knowledge which can be reached through technique or will-power and which leads to peace and certainty in a world of doubt and confusion. Holiness is in danger of becoming disengaged from the ordinary world in a search for direct experience of God as an end in itself. Such an approach offers very little renunciation and no radical commitment, merely tranquillity. Anxiety and conflict are seen as evil. This tends to go hand in hand with a socially unaware and escapist attitude.

While it is clear that the search for experience and contemplation as an end in itself may be self-regarding, the same may be true of shallow activism that has lost touch with its spiritual roots. While contemporary holiness should involve some degree of social awareness and even engagement in the face of a dehumanised world, it is also important to stress that engagement, or awareness or action, without contemplation is always in danger of remaining at the level of social theory.

Segundo Galilea, in his writings about the spirituality of liberation, speaks of a growth from an initial ethical response to social situations to a 'spiritual experience' properly so called. That is that the Christian will discover in the poor the reality of God's compassion and of Christ's humanity.[5] Thus, meeting the oppressed (as opposed merely to oppression in the abstract) becomes a source of spirituality and not simply of social theory. The Christian's response will not, therefore, be to create an ideology concerned merely with structural change but will also involve a contemplative awareness not only of the oppressed as individual and unique people (as opposed to a type or class) but also of the oppressors as people whom we are still called to love.

The call to holiness will also involve, as it has always done, a call to conversion. In an approach to holiness that does not settle merely for sacred action, but also involves secular commitment or a social dimension, such conversion will include conversion to justice. A model that has been suggested to describe this particular process is the call of the apostle Peter in the Gospel of Luke (5:1–11). There are three crucial elements or stages in this gospel story which fit well with a conversion to justice. The first is a new experience in which we see the world in a new way. This may be called 'conversion of the head'. There are, of course, serious obstacles even to this first stage. These are our presuppositions and unexamined values and unquestioned experiences of living. All these tend to support an analysis that does not call in question the structures on which I actually depend. The second element or stage, 'conversion of the feet', comes about when the new experience actually does reveal to me a reality of which I was previously unaware and which questions my assumptions. The third element or stage, 'conversion of the heart', is operative when the new experience, which has effectively questioned my assumptions, now demands a radical alteration in my life. I am compelled to do something, whether personally, socially or even politically.[6]

*Holiness or wholeness*

I have already touched briefly upon this third tension and I want to develop it here because I believe that along with, and closely related to, the tension between contemplation and social engagement this is one of the major contemporary spiritual problems.

Holiness may be described as the whole life of a person as directed towards God. By implication therefore, holiness involves not a part of life (let alone a denial of life) nor part of a person (let alone the denial of my unique personhood). Certainly salvation in the gospels is linked closely to healing (spiritual, psychic and physical) and therefore has something to do with wholeness. And yet, while I would maintain that growth in full humanity and growth in a relationship with God are intimately linked, I would also maintain that holiness is not identical with the perfectly psychologically balanced person.[7] It may be possible to see wholeness as of three kinds: the minimum necessary to function; a full human balance reached by a few and set as an ideal by, for example, educational theorists; the perfect balance of human and transcendent qualities. Certainly holiness will be present in the latter but may be present in either of the others – and even if the first 'functional wholeness' is not fully achieved.[8]

The history of the Christian community is full of people who have battled against temptation and failure to the end of their lives. Indeed, in my experience, growing closer to God involves a deepening awareness of the fact that we are far from perfect and far from sinless balanced, of course, with increasing trust and hope based on the realisation that we are not called and loved by God as a result of our efforts to make ourselves worthy. I would suggest that holiness is, in the experience of a great number of people, connected with failure and the acceptance of failure.

If this is the case, is therapy necessarily the road to holiness? Therapeutic theory undoubtedly underlines the importance of human growth but how do we understand growth? In Christian terms it is not sufficient to aim merely at adjustment, integration and authenticity. An unbalanced emphasis on individual growth, overlooks the fact that the Christian tradition of holiness has a communal dimension and derives from the foundational holiness of Christ. It would also be unbalanced to emphasise merely the faults and weakness of the individual rather than those of society. An uncritical adjustment to the expectations of society cannot be the final goal of holiness. Equally some contemporary spirituality so emphasises freedom from anguish and the attainment of inner peace that it may appear as the primary end in view.

It would, of course, be quite unfair to suggest that all therapists or all therapy theories fall into this trap. Some, such as R. D. Laing, would attack popular perceptions of sanity even among fellow psychiatrists. And someone like the American psychologist Rollo May also attacks a false religiosity that acts as a means of preventing real confrontation with evil by protecting us in an artificial world. He calls this 'pseudo-innocence', a state of being fixed in a childhood mentality that is mistaken for goodness.[9] A spirituality that screens out the ambiguities of experience and preserves innocence must also, in effect, preserve immaturity. It will tend towards an excessively externalised religiosity that bears a close resemblance to the picture of sanctity presented in the 'institutional' model of the Church which I mentioned previously.

It is important to remember that Christian life is not a question of invulnerability to the ravages of a society marred by a true lack of peace. It is possible to elevate the perfectly adjusted self to such a degree that this becomes an intolerably self-centred notion that contrasts strongly with the pain of a 'caring love' in a broken world. We must avoid the kind of 'individual adjustment' picture of holiness that is a substitute for social change, and is a way of reducing discontent. To live in love means ultimately to accept the risks of life and its threat to peace of mind.

The insights of psychology have, however, reminded us that sexuality is absolutely central to what it means to be human and therefore must be related to what it is to be holy. Sexuality needs to be integrated, ideally, with the remainder of human life and to be based, first of all, on acceptance. Yet, it must be admitted, spirituality and consequently understandings of holiness have frequently regarded sexuality as a hindrance to spiritual growth. It is worth emphasising therefore that, while human perfection and holiness are not entirely the same thing, the sexually immature person cannot simply bypass the quest for sexual integrity in the search for holiness.

## Conclusion

For all its value in emphasising that holiness is not a category distinct from the rest of human experience and living, the present tendency to over-identify holiness with wholeness raises the serious question of how far we can cope with the holiness of people whose emotional balance is extremely limited. Is it true that the love of God can only work in us if we remove guilt and fear altogether? I was very struck by a University Sermon at Oxford some years ago when it was suggested that part of our wholeness is an acknowledgement of our whole past which cannot be unmade. If part of that past is trauma, grace does not alter that truth. We have to acknowledge and accept our various emotional or physical diminishments. This, of itself, does not get in the way of holiness. That only becomes so if we use our diminishments as a defence against, for example, admitting guilt or as a way of justifying hopelessness.[10] I believe that this approach to holiness through and not despite our various diminishments is highly relevant to the issue of the relationship between holiness and social consciousness. We cannot experience 'solidarity' with the poor, socially or economically diminished unless we are also prepared to accept our own diminishment, our own inherent poverty. The 'wholeness' that is particular to the

Christian vision of holiness may therefore involve an identification, in my weakness, with the needs of the world in
its sickness.

In this, our model and our hope is the Cross of Jesus.
Christ in his loss and human diminishment gave himself
to the Father for all in complete poverty. My poverty
therefore becomes part of what I give rather than that
despite which I give! The poor of the earth, if they are to
hear the gospel of human and spiritual liberation, must do
so from those who understand their own poverty. Thus
holiness is nourished by a poor Christ living in poor
apostles, not by a fantasy of super-human health. All this
will be undermined if our popular and official perceptions
of holiness continue to edit all the struggle with failure and
sinfulness, and all the engagement with the brokenness of
the world, out of the process of becoming saints. It is the
idea of this element of struggle in discipleship that I now
want to develop in more depth.

1. A good example of such a study is *Saints and Society: the Two Worlds of Western Christendom, 1000–1700* by Donald Weinstein and Rudolph Bell (Chicago 1982). This examines 864 men, women and children and their *vitae* in a search for a composite picture of sanctity.
2. See, for example, Leonardo Boff, 'The Need for Political Saints' in *Cross Currents*, vol. xxx, 4 (Winter 1980–81), pp. 369–76. Also, Jon Sobrino, 'Political Holiness, a Profile' in *Concilium*, 163, 'Martyrdom Today' (Edinburgh/New York 1983), pp. 18–23.
3. Irene Bloomfield's paper in *Contact*, 61, 1978.
4. Avery Dulles, *Models of the Church* (Dublin 1976).
5. Segundo Galilea, 'The Spirituality of Liberation' in *The Way* (July 1985), pp. 186–94.
6. See Peter McVerry, 'Sin and Conversion' in *The Way* (July 1984), pp. 175–85, to which I am indebted for some of these ideas.
7. For a useful summary of the holiness/wholeness debate see Kenneth Leech, *The Social God* (London 1981), chapter 7.
8. The British psychologist Brendan Callaghan summarises many of these points well in his article, 'Holiness and wholeness' in *The Month* (August 1980), pp. 263–66.
9. Rollo May, *Power and Innocence* (New York 1972), *passim*.
10. Rowan Williams, the University Sermon, preached at the University Church of St Mary the Virgin, Oxford on Sunday, 1 November 1981.

# 3
# A Spirituality of Struggle

Christian holiness, I have suggested, is not a search simply for tranquillity and invulnerability. Christian tradition has always emphasised that a kind of 'holy discontent' and struggle is an essential part of the journey towards fulfilment, towards God. Spirituality should neither shield us from the darker side of human experience by protecting us in an artificial world nor preserve a kind of innocence that is, in effect, human and spiritual immaturity. To seek the face of the living God is a risky business and part of that risk is that the search will bring us, inevitably, face to face with our own reality which includes weakness and failure. We desire God, we desire to love and we desire to reach the fullness of our humanity and yet we find, sooner or later, that our desire is an ambiguous matter. In the first chapter of the Gospel of John, Jesus asks the disciples of John the Baptist: 'What do you seek?' 'What are you looking for?' If we were to put ourselves in that gospel scene and hear the question addressed to ourselves it would be easy enough to respond with the 'appropriate' answers. 'It is your face, O Lord, that I seek; hide not your face' (Ps. 27:8). But are our desires that clear, our hearts that undivided?

Spirituality is concerned with coming to terms with divided hearts, with the proper channelling of desire. Spirituality, therefore, has to do with getting our confused desires in some kind of order. For this reason those seeking to know God and to be known have invariably developed theories about those practices which will be effective means to assist the deepening of knowledge of self and of God. The traditional Christian word for this has been 'asceticism' from the Greek word *askesis* or discipline and training.

It is first of all a way of knowledge, of realisation of what there is within us that prevents us from gaining what our hearts most deeply desire and secondly it seeks ways round these barriers.

Discipline alone or for its own sake undoubtedly kills the spirit. On the other hand ideals or good intentions, unaccompanied by an experience of struggle, seem eventually to reach a dead end. A problem, therefore, is always how to achieve a proper balance. Another is that the traditional language of asceticism can appear so negative and dehumanising: self-denial, mortification, penance and detachment or indifference.[1]

'Those who belong to Christ Jesus have crucified the flesh with its passions and desires' (Gal. 5:24). The tendency to a literal application of this apparent call to deny the flesh, passion or desires contrasts with contemporary thinking in the Church and society. The teaching of St Paul (in the verse from Galatians just quoted for example) and much of the Christian tradition have been accused of treating the human body simply as a prison, pleasure as self-indulgence, and the world as a 'vale of tears' which we have to transcend or merely survive. Where, in all this, is there a place for the proper enjoyment of God's gift of creation? Is it not the case that 'asceticism' is irredeemably associated either with an unreal distinction between the 'spiritual' and material that is sub-Christian or with an unbalanced emphasis on the 'next world' which prevents any commitment to time or to creation? When people say, for example, that 'He's a real ascetic' it is all too often shorthand for 'What a kill-joy!'

*An ambiguous inheritance*

Thus, the tradition of Christian spirituality with regard to asceticism presents real difficulties. It is not an exaggeration to suggest that, in medieval perceptions of sanctity, ascetical practices played a central role.[2] Miracles and strange powers, after all, were the hall-mark of witches and necromancers as well as saints. Asceticism was an important sign-value which differentiated the saintly from the demonic. However, despite some fascination among their contemporaries with penitential athleticism, saints were also respected for their humility in the search for perfection and in the performance of ascetical exercises.

In the minds both of practitioners and observers, asceticism was concerned essentially with a mastery over bodily demands. The struggle was to eradicate the last vestiges of worldly honour and regard for self, whether spiritual or bodily. The divine will was felt to be revealed most effectively through people who were purified by asceticism, or, more exactly, who were immune to the temptations of the flesh. This was so precisely because the body was seen as the primary context for the battle between will and uncontrolled impulses. The *sine qua non* of bodily control was sexual renunciation, and chastity was a universally understood symbol of a much wider rejection of the flesh and the world. Popular wisdom as well as religious theory tended to identify sexual relations as the dividing line between innocence and worldliness and here there could be no degrees or compromises.

Some medieval notions of asceticism that survived until relatively recently had a great deal to do with the expiation of guilt. This could be highly personal. So, for example, Elena di Udine is recorded as having chastised every member of her body in turn as she recalled the offences of each. The phenomenon of a personal burden of guilt and the desire for expiation is very striking even among the wider public. Lay fraternities and religious processions practised flagellation, especially from the fourteenth century onwards. These popular movements were part of a deep sensitivity about personal responsibility for the moral condition of society. No doubt this was, in part, provoked by the prevalence of plague and thus the sense that God was judging a community unmindful of its Christian duties. It should not surprise us that much the same atmosphere seems to pervade some of the apocalytic 'visions' that are increasingly common in our own era around the world. Calls to fasting and penance to combat the forces of evil and to make atonement for sin seem to increase in proportion to the degree of insecurity felt about the condition of the world – whether moral decay, political threat (most usually communism), or even the decline of the Church since the Vatican Council.

While the expiation of guilt seems fairly central to medieval asceticism, it was not always conceived in purely individual terms. Catherine of Siena practised austerities partly to atone for the evil of her times, the sins of Church and society, and disciplined by her penance was able to spend remarkable energy in working for the reform of the Church. Asceticism was often associated with a reversal of prevalent social values. Thus the friars sought to reverse the less fortunate moral effects of commercial expansion and the emergence of an urban bourgeoisie and to call the Church back from a preoccupation with worldly power. So penitential ascetics suffered not only for their own sins but were advocates, intercessors and protectors expiating the sins of all.

### An unbalanced asceticism

The less healthy side of the medieval view that 'professional' ascetics had a social role was that they all too easily became surrogates for those members of the Church who had too little time or inclination to pursue spiritual perfection for themselves. This reinforced the distinction, which had crept into the Church over the preceding centuries, between a moderate asceticism appropriate to all the baptised disciples of Christ (works of charity, prayer and observation of the fasts of the Church) and the monastic counsels seen as the way *par excellence* to the higher degrees of holiness. In other words, asceticism was an elitist concept. Although monastic life undoubtedly contributed to the spiritual life of all members of the Church by inspiration, it also tended gradually to have the negative effect of minimising the value of lay life and of marriage in particular.

This elitism is at least one of the reasons for the sixteenth-century Reformers' rejection of the ascetic ideal and monasticism in general. However Luther also objected to traditional ideas of asceticism on the grounds that they placed greater emphasis on 'human works' as necessary for salvation than on faith, and underplayed redemption

as pure gift. Sacrifice has an inherent Christian value but
we also need to remember that our relationship with God,
as Jesus made abundantly clear on several occasions, does
not consist in offering sacrifices. Rather, the Christian life
is a process of allowing ourselves to be drawn into the
basic sacrifice of Christ. An unbalanced ascetical view can
so easily lead to the substitution of *sacrifices* for Christ's
unique sacrifice.

Some older spirituality reveals a sense that human
passions get in the way of growth in the Spirit and consequently that asceticism is a process of curbing passion.
Although Western writers placed less emphasis than those
of the East on the virtue of *apatheia* or passionless calm it
is nonetheless the case that passionlessness, in practice,
played a significant role in the traditional understanding
of asceticism. 'Passion' is a rich and, simultaneously, an
ambiguous word. Because it is ambiguous it is dangerous
territory. Different, contradictory, images are conjured up:
love at its most intense, or strong commitment, but also
violent anger or uncontrolled desire. Thus we often prefer
to forget or bury passion in the safe and deep recesses
of our person. Here, the negative aspects of passion are,
apparently, out of harm's way but its positive power is
chained as well.

In a meeting of people involved in active ministry in the
Church, clergy and lay, we were discussing various models
of pastoral guidance. One of the unhelpful ones was 'the
case of the plaster saint' – the disembodied pastor/
counsellor who gives the impression of being 'above these
things' when talking to a client. Apart from making it
pretty difficult for the other person to be honest about
ambiguous feelings, such a model tends to reinforce the
sense that strong feelings or emotions of any kind are less
than perfect or a sign of weakness: the ideal Christian
remains cool and collected and preferably untouched under
all circumstances. On a more everyday level, how many of
us I wonder have received the impression that feelings do
not matter in prayer or, worse, that they get in the way –
particularly 'negative' ones such as anger? Equally outside
prayer many of us in everyday life have difficulty in owning
strong feelings such as anger, let alone expressing them

openly to other people. Such feelings are the cause of guilt-feelings rather than possible channels for growth and movement.

Passion, for all its dangers, needs uncaging if we are to move towards completeness as human beings and if our walking with Christ in faith is to pass beyond the cerebral and the emotionally anaemic. The trouble with the ambiguity of passion is that we sense that we cannot get it in order on our own and so run away not only from our humanity but in a sense from God as well. Metropolitan Anthony (Bloom) once commented that an encounter with God was to enter the cave of a tiger rather than to play with a pussy-cat.[3] To travel into the deeper reaches of our nature where passion lies is much the same. But it is there, in the ensuing struggle, that we can meet God and where the starkness of faith may confront us. As we shall see, the origins of Christian asceticism in the desert tradition of the early centuries of the Church included a deep awareness of this fact. In wrestling with our ambiguous passions we too can learn to say 'Into your hands I commit my spirit'. Only in letting ourselves enter that darkness will losing ourselves in God become a possibility.

An ascetical view of the Christian life has also frequently meant a rejection of normal human tendencies and of materiality. It is hardly surprising, therefore, that asceticism came to be seen both as unattractive and as not expressive of the fundamental Christian belief in the Incarnation – that God, in Jesus, entered the human condition and raised it into the divine. To talk of an incarnate God presupposes a fundamentally optimistic (though not naive) view of human nature. Too often the tendency has been to assume that humans are radically and inherently bad.[4] Paul Verghese, the Indian Syrian Orthodox theologian, quite rightly castigates this view: 'Regard the flesh, the body, matter as evil or even inferior, and one has already begun the deviation from Christian truth.'[5]

A spirituality that seriously neglects the body and matter is open to the danger of the abandonment of the essentially materialistic and historical character of the Christian spiritual path (a kind of contemporary version of the ancient heresy of gnosticism).[6] 'By affirming that all "meaning", every assertion about the significance of life and reality, must be judged by reference to a brief succession of contingent events in Palestine, Christianity . . . closed off the path to "timeless truth". That is to say, it becomes increasingly difficult in the Christian world to see the ultimately important human experience as an escape into the transcendent, a flight out of history and the flesh.'[7] If matter is seen as the source of sin and impurity, the spiritual person needs to reject the physical and the sexual. The human life of Jesus is, practically speaking, irrelevant. Spirituality shifts towards interiority, the inner life of the disciple.

The word 'spirituality' derives from the Greek *pneuma* and *pneumatikos* (spirit and spiritual) in the Pauline letters. It is therefore vital to grasp that, in Pauline theology, 'spiritual' is not contrasted with 'material' but rather with anything (including the mind) which is opposed to the spirit of God. The contrast is, therefore, between two attitudes to life. The Pauline understanding of human nature is no basis for a flesh-denying asceticism or a contrast between 'physical' and 'spiritual', 'body' and 'soul'.

The Incarnation is more than an assertion about the human nature of Christ; it is a governing principle of the Christian life, of God's way of relating to the world. The consequence of an incarnational spirituality is that we should not fear or despise the body but see it as the handiwork of God. Fear of the body overflows into a fear of sexuality or bodily pleasure of any kind. Because sex was associated with the body and the body with the Fall it was felt that sex could never occur without impurity. It is hardly surprising, therefore, that fear of sexual temptations or sins of the flesh was the primary reason for much of the extreme ascetical practice recorded in the lives of saints.

## A return to origins

It has been suggested that the origin of asceticism in the early Syriac communities was simply a continuation (though subject to certain exaggerations) of the ideal of *discipleship* of the poor, homeless and celibate Jesus. So, in its roots, Christian asceticism is another word for the

quality of absoluteness or total response in true discipleship.[8] This emphasis on discipleship in the origins of
Christian asceticism provides a helpful balance to some
later deviations which we have inherited, and so I want to
concentrate, briefly, on the early tradition as a way of
moving towards a reassessment of asceticism and struggle
in the contemporary Christian journey.[9]

The early desert fathers and mothers withdrew into the
wilderness as a symbol of their desire to enter the wasteland
of the spirit. The desert, as twentieth-century writers such
as T. E. Lawrence and Antoine de Saint-Exupéry have
eloquently described, is a place of stark simplicity from
which normal human aids and comforts are absent. The
emptiness of the desert is a place of testing through temptation, of stripping and gradual detachment. The loss of
familiar signposts and supports becomes a symbol of the
essentially pilgrim nature of the Christian life.

The life of those fathers and mothers was one of radical
simplicity. Certainly there were those who went beyond
the simple into greater fasts for example, but the desert
ideal was not in essence super-human or a matter of spiritual and ascetical gymnastics. The desert tradition emphasised the vital importance of humility – without it asceticism could be extremely dangerous. Certainly the desert
encapsulated a life of continual striving or struggle but not
of excessive effort. Anthony the Great compared excess to
the abuse of a bow and arrow: 'If we push ourselves beyond
measure we will break; it is right for us from time to time
to relax our efforts.'[10] Struggle was a way of training the
whole person to understand the nature of evil desires in
order to be rid of them.

In other words, the desert solitaries sought self-know-
ledge and discernment above all. 'Some have afflicted their
bodies by asceticism, but they lack discernment, and so
they are far from God.'[11] The Abba Poemen taught that
discernment was the most important gift. 'Many of our
fathers have become very courageous in asceticism, but in
fineness of perception there are very few.'[12] Abba Syncletica
went further and suggested that asceticism may in fact be
'demonic tyranny'. How then can we distinguish this from

'divine and royal asceticism'? It was in its quality of balance. 'Lack of proportion always corrupts.'[13]

It is important to grasp that asceticism was not an end in itself; the aim was not penance but God. Asceticism, as struggle, combatted those forces which take people away from acquiring fullness of life in Christ. Its basic purpose, therefore, was a simultaneous decrease in self-reliance and self-assertiveness, and growth in dependence on and trust in the mercy of God. It was an instrument of deep inner conversion rather than the infliction of pain on a body rejected as sinful. The solitaries were not world-denying gnostics nor escapists from human relationships. Charity was the pivot of all their work and the test of their way of life. The desert fathers and mothers had a deep understanding of the connection between a person's spiritual and natural life and it was for this reason, not because of rejection, that they stressed the right-ordering of the body.

Warfare with the forces of evil was a major concern of the desert tradition. The wilderness was not a place where you went to escape from temptation but precisely to struggle with it. Certainly the passions should be put in order, but desert spirituality was not a recipe for invulnerability to passion. Continual struggle was vital. One father prayed for deliverance from passion but another, more senior, advised him to ask for his passions back in order to regain the afflictions that bred humility so as to continue to make progress.

The asceticism of the desert contrasts strongly with comfortable and comforting versions of Christianity. 'In the desert we face our own weaknesses and the perils which they involve . . . The desert is supremely the place of trial and, because of this, the place of holiness and of transformation.'[14] The main value of the desert teaching on asceticism is the need to detach ourselves from false ideas of the self and from excessive dependence on created things in order to stand before God in simplicity. The emphasis on struggle is a salutary reminder that we are called to die to the safe and conventional (just as the solitaries withdrew from an urban Christianity that was increasingly socially conformist). If some contemporary spirituality seems to view tranquillity and experience as ends in themselves, the desert tradition of ascesis underlines that to meet God involves a launching out from the familiar into a strange land in the spirit of Abraham.

## Denial and fulfilment

Earlier I quoted the Letter to the Galatians where it speaks of Christian disciples as those who have crucified the flesh. The flesh that we are to crucify is not our humanity however but that selfish part of ourselves that leads us to be out of harmony with other people and the whole of creation. In this disharmony we confuse self-indulgence with enjoyment, the pride of the Pharisees with legitimate self-esteem. By not appreciating our spiritual dimension we move from a profound vision of our dignity to one where life is no more than an uncritical satisfaction of desire. To be fully human is, as St Paul saw, much more than this. The asceticism of 'crucifying the flesh with its passions and desires' is the process of freeing ourselves from the prison of selfishness.

Although asceticism is fundamentally about inner conversion we must nevertheless recover a spirituality of life-style. Without this there is a danger of empty interiority or a spiritualisation of the Christian life. Simply to reintroduce such practices as Friday abstinence does not answer this need, for they can so easily be thoroughly individualistic and unrelated to our lives and attitudes as a whole. Conversion is never automatic nor instantaneous but involves a continuous struggle throughout life to respond to God with a radical and absolute 'Yes'. Few of us can ever say 'Yes' in this total sense. Reflection on certain elements of our life-style, or certain actions may bring a realisation that they express deep fear of the unknown implications of saying this 'Yes' wholeheartedly. A valid asceticism helps us to bring together gradually into a coherent whole what we say we believe and the way we behave. As an example, to say that we believe that the Christian gospel implies justice to our neighbour, and that our 'neighbour' is every person, also points, for some of us, towards accepting a drop in material standards so that others may have sufficient. We can find ourselves resisting

this quite fiercely with such apparently reasonable phrases
as 'We must work to bring them up to our level, not reduce
ourselves to theirs'.

Contemporary understandings of Christian life-style
emphasise its communal aspects. Asceticism, therefore, will
involve a reordering of relationships. Jesus entered a fabric
of human relationships that was radically disordered.
'Sharing all he was' may be said to be at the heart of
Jesus' response and 'sharing all we are' is at the heart of
discipleship. A Christian asceticism will include a dedi-
cation to the needs and sufferings of others. Increasingly,
in a world dominated on the one hand by material acquisi-
tiveness and on the other by acute poverty, people talk of
frugality as perhaps the most significant Christian virtue
for the end of the century. The tradition of asceticism has
much to say, surely, about the necessity of simplicity and
austerity in the midst of wealth. There is a recovery of
interest in fasting precisely in this context.

## Struggle and discipleship

Asceticism is a continuation of discipleship. At the centre
of discipleship is struggle. It involves engagement in the
irreconcilable conflict between God and Mammon (Matt.
6:24) which is the central element of the Gospel as
expounded in the Matthean Sermon on the Mount. No one
can serve two masters, can respond adequately to God
with a divided heart. Intimacy with and response to God
is linked inextricably to a repudiation of Mammon.
Mammon is more than mere material possessions. It is a
subtle inner attitude that seeks to be, by acquiring and
possessing. This is most graphically illustrated by much
contemporary magazine and television advertising: 'No one
has any doubts about a man in a . . . suit', 'Driving a . . .
says a lot about who you are', and so on. We struggle
continually towards an inner and outward freedom from
the kind of self-centredness that undermines the validity of
our prayer and action. This self-forgetfulness is nothing
less than Jesus' characteristic response to God and the
world: humility, rejection of power (except that of love),
obedience to God's will and acceptance of failure. It is not

a negative rejection of being human but a realisation that to be fully human is always to move outwards towards others. To gain life by giving it.

If we turn to the tradition of the *Spiritual Exercises*, we see that Ignatius of Loyola did not fight futile battles against imaginary enemies such 'matter' or 'the body'. At one of the most decisive moments of the Exercises, Ignatius confronts the person who seeks to follow Christ more closely with two conflicting 'Standards' or attitudes: either riches, which produce 'pride and vainglory', or poverty which builds up the Kingdom of God through humility, the fruit of suffering.[15] By suffering Ignatius does not mean arbitrary penance or a denial of the good things of human life nor on the other hand the temptation to identify, in an over-glib way, our normal day-to-day frustrations with a radical taking up our cross daily. What is meant at root by the traditional words 'self-denial' is the continual struggle to 'take up the cross' of unconditioned discipleship; to respond with increasing depth, generosity and openness to the Lord's call. We need to look as honestly as we can at our real deep desires, and what gets in the way of a more wholehearted response to God's love. The key to understanding Christian suffering, or 'poverty' and 'struggle', is to remember that Jesus did not embrace any of these experiences as ends in themselves but as the means to spread the Kingdom of God.

Christian asceticism, therefore, is orientated towards the fullness of love, towards service, to greater availability and to the freedom 'to seek and find the will of God' without the burden of those apparent needs, fears, and conflicts within us that stand in the way of what we most deeply and truly desire. When Ignatius Loyola speaks of people 'making themselves indifferent' he is not talking about a denial of human feelings or proper needs, but he is concerned about the freedom to choose the best means to respond to a loving God and to work for a world where this will be the guiding principle of progress.[16] In scriptural terms this freedom, and the struggle that is necessary for it to become operative, may be expressed in the openness of Mary to the Angel's message (Luke 1:38), Jesus' perfect receptivity to the will of his Father (Luke 22:42), the disciple's trust in providence that frees him or her from an excessive concern for life's necessities (Matt. 6:25ff), and the classical expression in the Letter to the Philippians (3, 7–16): 'I believe that nothing can happen that will outweigh the supreme advantage of knowing Christ Jesus my Lord. For him I have accepted the loss of everything . . . All I want is to know Christ.'

Christian asceticism or struggle is concerned with self-forgetting love in the pattern of Jesus' life and death, not with a belief that suffering in itself is, perversely, a good thing. Equally, to follow the pattern of Jesus involves a growing dependence on the power of God, based on an ever-deepening trust. We are too often burdened with a sense of guilt because our own capacity to respond and to move seems so limited. But such guilt is a trap. Perhaps the greatest 'asceticism' or struggle is to learn, slowly and painfully, to let go of the desire to succeed, to be in control or to make ourselves worthy and acceptable to God – in short, to perfect ourselves. Gethsemane reminds us that, just as for Jesus, so for us the struggle to entrust ourselves, our future and our hopes to a loving God remains with us throughout life. The cross is the greatest sign that the strength of God to transform us is shown best in the midst of our weakness (2 Cor. 12). I have found that this very human problem transcends the boundaries of denominations and supposed Catholic or Protestant emphases about grace and free will! An important key to our understanding of asceticism, therefore, is to recover the richness of a theology and spirituality of the Cross.

1.  See entries for 'asceticism', 'detachment', 'indifference' and 'mortification' in Gordon Wakefield (ed), *A Dictionary of Christian Spirituality* (London 1984).
2.  There are numerous examples of medieval attitudes to asceticism in Donald Weinstein and Rudolph Bell, *Saints and Society: the Two Worlds of Western Christendom, 1000–1700* (Chicago 1982). See especially pp. 153–57 in the section 'Who was a saint?'
3.  See Anthony Bloom, *School for Prayer* (London 1970), pp. xv–xvi.
4.  For the implications of the doctrine of the Incarnation for spirituality see Kenneth Leech, *The Social God* (London 1981), chapter 3. Leech uses his arguments to justify a socially concerned Chris-

tianity but his approach is equally relevant to our understanding of asceticism.

5. Paul Verghese is now Paulos Mar Gregorios, Metropolitan of Delhi and the North. He is quoted in Leech, op.cit., p.25.
6. For a further discussion of incarnational spirituality see Kenneth Leech, *True God* (London 1985), pp. 242–50.
7. Rowan Williams, *The Wound of Knowledge* (London 1981), pp. 1–2.
8. See Robert Murray, 'The Features of the Earliest Christian Asceticism' in *Christian Spirituality: Essays in Honour of Gordon Rupp*, ed. Peter Brooks (London 1975), pp. 65–77.
9. For a helpful general survey of desert spirituality see Leech, *True God*, ch.5. See also Benedicta Ward's three translations of the sayings and lives of the desert solitaries: *Wisdom of the Desert Fathers* (Fairacres, Oxford, 1981) cited as *Wisdom; The Sayings of the Desert Fathers* (London 1981) cited as *Sayings; The Lives of the Desert Fathers* (London 1980).
10. Quoted in Ward, *Wisdom*, p. xv.
11. Ward, *Sayings*, p. 3.
12. Ward, *Sayings*, p. 182.
13. Ward, *Sayings*, p. 233.
14. Leech, *True God*, p. 154.
15. See Louis Puhl (ed.), *The Spiritual Exercises of St Ignatius of Loyola* (Chicago 1951), sections 135–47.
16. *Exercises*, 23.

# 4
# Discipleship and the Cross

A residual Christian consciousness among the British public frequently expresses itself at the traditional festivals of Christmas and Good Friday. Congregations at carol services and Midnight Mass, or at the Three Hours Service and Solemn Liturgy of Good Friday are swelled by many people who do not darken the doors of any church during the remainder of the year. Apart from nostalgia and perhaps a response to the poetry of such festivals there seems to be an instinctive recognition that these two occasions touch the human condition in a special way. A birth and a death – Incarnation and Passion – both offer some kind of hope in a darkened world which still speaks to the desire of an 'unchurched' society that life be more than the obvious events and struggles of daily living.

In a sense Christmas and Good Friday, Incarnation and Cross, are two poles from which to view the meaning of the good news of Jesus Christ. Too often, sadly, they have been seen as alternative perspectives rather than as complementary ones. There is some truth in the suggestion that Catholic spirituality has placed more emphasis on the Incarnation and Protestant spirituality on the Cross. I have already described how a spirituality of struggle or asceticism is at the heart of discipleship but needs to be placed in the context of a proper understanding of the Cross. In reflecting on the relationship between the Cross and spirituality I want to concentrate my attention on the spirituality of St Ignatius Loyola (and especially on his *Spiritual Exercises*). This is precisely because a great number of people have found in the Ignatian approach to the Christian life an archetype of incarnational spirituality that highlights the value of everyday human experiences and the process of more and more 'finding God in all things'.[1] There is certainly a great deal of truth in this perception but to stop here, to isolate the 'incarnational' aspects, would be to miss other central emphases in St Ignatius's thinking.

Before going any further we should be aware that the Exercises are not intended to be read as a 'spiritual classic'! The book is a series of notes to aid a spiritual director. The Spiritual Exercises are a structured but very flexible retreat-experience. Traditionally, in their full form, they last approximately thirty days. However St Ignatius's introductory remarks allow for various forms of adaptation, including the possibility of undertaking them in daily life without the need to withdraw from family and work. In this case the duration depends on the circumstances of the person and in practice may be between six months and a year.

To attempt to describe the structure and dynamic of the Exercises in a few sentences is difficult and open to the criticism of over-simplification, but broadly the experience of the Exercises is divided into four periods or 'weeks'. In practice these 'weeks' are not rigidly seven days long but vary according to the needs of the individual retreatant. The 'weeks' express identifiable stages in a dynamic within the Exercises. The process begins with prayerful reflection on the love and creativity of God and on the purpose and direction of my life. Such reflection leads quite naturally to an awareness of what prevents me responding freely to God's love – sinfulness. The latter is the focus of the first 'week' proper. A realisation that God's love and merciful forgiveness enables me to respond to God's call leads into the second 'week' contemplations on the life and mission of the Jesus of history and on to the call to be with him in mission. Inevitably this leads to a sense that to respond wholeheartedly to Jesus involves the Cross, and this is the focus of the third of the 'weeks'. The final, fourth 'week' seeks to share the joy of the risen Christ and the concluding 'Contemplation to attain the love of God' is both a way of praying, of 'finding God in all things', and a bridge back from the retreat into ordinary life.

Naturally we have to face the fact that in certain crucial

respects Ignatius's perspective is different from our own. Unless we adopt a crude 'textual fundamentalism' this will surely raise important questions about the relationship between contemporary perspectives and that of the Exercises and indeed of any classical Christian spiritual text. To put matters simply (some might say, excessively so) we have to accept both the insights of a tradition as it has come down to us *and* our own insights so that a new understanding is reached. But at the end of the day our *use* of any spiritual classic (as opposed merely to our understanding of it) must not simply reflect the situation of the original writer but our own context too. We have to interpret in the light of our own historical situation a text that was written in another. In this way a text comes alive for us instead of remaining merely an antique from the past to be admired.

Central to the experience of the Exercises is a choice, an option for Christ and to share with him in building the Kingdom of God. Such choice necessarily involves struggle and even suffering on the road to inner and outward freedom and to a discipleship that consists of being with a Christ who is poor and has nowhere to lay his head and is associated with the despised and powerless of the earth. Arguably all Christian spirituality, insofar as it is specifically Christian, is 'imitation of Christ', that is, living out our human existence in the light of Christ. In this context St Ignatius Loyola subjects all Christian prayer and action to one common test of authenticity: 'self-abnegation', or, in more positive language, self-giving.[2] For all genuine spirituality flows from the spirit of the Cross – the self-emptying in love of the crucified Christ. Both contemplation and action can be undermined by self-centredness, St Ignatius's reaction to over-enthusiastic contemplatives among the Jesuits who desired to spend more and more time in meditation was that they should apply their enthusiasm more to their calling to give themselves in selfless service of God and their fellow humans, for then it would not take them long to find God. Perhaps in our contemporary enthusiasm for meditation we need to recover this doctrine of self-giving or self-forgetfulness as a central criterion for testing spirituality. For without this movement outwards from ourselves, *kenosis*, there is a real danger of delusion with self-centred introspection parading as contemplativity and restless activity as working for the Kingdom. In our perfectly valid contemporary concern to get away from the bleakness and negative feel of some inherited spirituality and to return to the experience of joy at the unconditioned love that God shows us, we must nonetheless not lose touch with the hard gospel demand for taking up the cross as a condition of true discipleship. We live in an age which can give the impression of wanting to turn its back on struggle and to ignore the fact that all growth inevitably involves some apparent loss. Christ can seem more attractive without his Cross.

The Incarnation and the Cross can only be understood in terms of each other. This is true both of theology and spirituality in general and also of St Ignatius's thinking specifically. Thus in the Exercises the Third Week, which focuses on praying the Passion, reveals more deeply what is implied in the Contemplation on the Incarnation at the beginning of the Second Week. Theologically, to view the Incarnation from the standpoint of the Cross provides a different perspective on the nature of God's engagement with human experience and indeed on the very *nature of God*. Again to view the Cross from the perspective of the Incarnation and Jesus's life as a whole situates the Passion within a wider context and thus moves us away from a sense that the Cross symbolises merely arbitrary and meaningless suffering. The Cross is the inevitable consequence of God's engagement with a world that is ambiguous, sinful (not merely the sins of individuals but a 'sinful world'), and is marred by conflict and injustice and so out of harmony, as it were, with itself. The Cross, too, is a sign that this disharmony can be overcome, that hope is not merely an abstract virtue but a realistic vision. That, in the words of Julian of Norwich, despite all appearances 'all shall be well and all manner of thing shall be well' in the power of the redemptive love of God.

Contemporary criticism of much traditional Christian spirituality often includes the accusation of individualism. Certainly St Ignatius, for example, emphasises the experience of the individual, the uniqueness of each person's

journey. His Spiritual Exercises are full of references to the
need for a spiritual director to respect this uniqueness and
to adapt the retreat-experience to the situation of each
person. However, even in St Ignatius's own terms this is
no excuse for a purely *individualistic* interpretation of the
Exercises. It has been pointed out, for example, that within
each part of the Exercises there is a definite movement
from the general to the particular, from the cosmic to
the individual. The individual's prayer, while focusing on
personal experience, is therefore situated within a wider
context from the start. Thus Ignatius's consideration of sin
moves from its 'cosmic' nature (the angels) through various
stages so that the consideration of personal sinfulness is
the last element to be focused upon. Before contemplating
the life of Christ and our call to be with Christ (what
Ignatius calls the Second Week), Ignatius invites us to see
the world and all its people through the eyes of God in
Trinity. The pain of the world therefore forms a kind of
backdrop to the week as a whole.

In the search for a less individualistic spirituality and
for greater social awareness, the recovery of a theology of
the Cross offers some of the clearest perspectives. Put
simply, the various contemporary theologies of the Cross
all emphasise, in their different ways, that to view the
Passion of Christ in purely 'vertical' terms without a 'horizontal' dimension would be to empty the Cross of ultimate
meaning. What I propose to do, therefore, is to highlight
some of the most significant elements of the contemporary
recovery of a theology of the Cross and to ask what these
may contribute to our rereading of spirituality and of the
Ignatian Exercises in particular.

### The Cross in contemporary perspective

Until fairly recently, theological reflection on the Cross
was infrequent and when it happened it rarely showed
the Cross (and thus a God who did not simply become
incarnate but who is a 'crucified God') as something
that embodies the particularity of Christian faith. The
tradition we inherited tended to elaborate a mystique of
suffering and sorrow. In reaction some recent theology and

spirituality responded with an emphasis on the Resurrection as the paradigm of liberty and joy which, it was felt, had been understressed in a traditional piety of the Cross. Interestingly, the recovery of the Cross has frequently been associated with theologies concerned with social change.[3] For these the Resurrection remains the paradigm of liberation but the Cross is no longer seen purely as suffering. The viability of the Resurrection is involved intimately with the experience of the Cross; without the Cross the Resurrection is in danger of becoming pure utopianism. Sobrino argues that we tend to dilute the Cross because we suffer from a post-Resurrection view of Jesus' death. Concretely this implies several things. Firstly the *scandal* of the Cross is lost in a mollifying tendency towards death and abandonment by God. Then the Cross is reduced to some 'mystery of God's wonderful design' that fails to produce a crisis for our knowledge of God. Finally it is very difficult to recognise God *in* the Cross of Jesus for the latter's divinity seems suspended. To focus on the glory of God is important of course, but the vulnerability of Christ on the Cross is also a vital source of knowledge about God which can lead us to a deep sense that self-giving love[4] (in other words, vulnerability), and not just power, may in fact transform us and our world. Apparent failure, and even suffering, may of course merely trap us in a sense of hopelessness, powerlessness and pointlessness. The God who is revealed in the Cross of Jesus is one who offers the vision, the possibility of reaching the fullness of our humanity (glory) through and not merely despite the apparently destructive experiences of our lives.

Theologians engaged with this recovery of the Cross have attempted to overcome two obstacles that stand in the way of grasping the profundity of Christ's Passion: its isolation from the concrete history of the human Jesus, and its isolation from our ways of understanding God. A number of recent thinkers have suggested that this 'reconstruction' of the theology of God, of our understanding of Jesus and of human existence arises largely from a major shift during this century in the way we can grasp the world and Christ's work of redemption. As I noted earlier in my first chapter, a number of factors, involving both developments in human knowledge, recent historical events and social trends, have undermined the world view that we have inherited and thus mark a decisive and distinctive break with much theology of the past. These factors have entered into the thinking of contemporary men and women to a profound degree, often in an unreflected way.[5]

In this context, a theology of the Cross replaces the certainties and self-reliance of an over-confident Christianity with a theology that arises from the newer experience of powerlessness and weakness and the sinfulness of so many human structures. Our confidence in the power of human beings to solve their own problems has been severely challenged, and this points to a radical need for salvation from this condition – not merely the *pardoning of particular sins* but the *destruction of the very power of sin in itself* at the centre of the human condition. Attention once again has to be given to the nature of hope -- of hoping against hope. Only those who have experienced the Cross in a radical way can really formulate such a Christian hope. For Christians believe that God has intervened decisively in human history and yet come in weakness not power. God in Jesus Christ redeems the 'hells' of human experience. From the Cross of Jesus comes the power of the Spirit to liberate all humanity from every condition of slavery. Current theologies of the Cross would therefore make our way of understanding Jesus Christ (our Christology) the cornerstone of theology, see the heart of Christology in the Cross, and see the very being of God as revealed in this death. Thus the Cross becomes the revelation both of the nature of God and of a world in need of redemption. Such writers as Moltmann and von Balthasar emphasise more strongly the relationship between the inner life of God and the death of the human Jesus at a particular point in our history,[6] while liberation theologians relate the Cross to the struggle for liberation and justice (redemption of, rather than from, the world).[7]

I would now like to focus briefly on three of the central themes of contemporary thinking on the Cross and how they affect our spirituality.

## 1. A crucified God

To love means to be vulnerable since a person suffers in the sufferings of the beloved. In freely creating humanity out of love, God is made vulnerable. Both Moltmann and von Balthasar speak of Jesus' experience of the silence and absence of God on the Cross.[8] He reaches the darker depths of human experience where we feel ourselves to be alienated from God – essentially the sense of sinfulness. Von Balthasar relates Christ's abandonment on the Cross to the inner life of the Trinity.

The very being of God is selfless love with all that this implies. To speak of God as the changeless one has an important element of truth but stated so baldly can easily lead to misunderstanding – making God into one who is not affected by what happens and whose essential condition is *apathy* or painlessness and non-suffering. In contrast, contemporary theological reflection on the Cross seeks to overcome the real difficulty presented by this traditional 'apathetic' theology of God as immutable and essentially uninvolved. The *pathos* or suffering of God is stressed for, as Bonhoeffer suggests, 'only a suffering God can help'.[9] An apathetic approach is felt to distort a properly biblical notion of God who loves, desires, is angry and jealous. Jesus on the Cross is not therefore an invulnerable God, rather the Cross is the vulnerability of God: revealing the extent of love by letting us know the extent of God's suffering for us. Put another way, the Cross is the fulfilment of the prohibition against idols or false images of God whose transcendence is now reformulated in terms of suffering love rather than remote power.

## 2. A world in need of redemption

If the Cross forces us to re-examine our understanding of God, so it must also force us to question a distorted view of redemption. Firstly the Cross was not accidental; merely God's surprised reaction to an unexpected Fall. There must have been a 'Calvary in the heart of God' before there was a Calvary in Jerusalem.[10] If we say, therefore, that the nature of God is to be a suffering God, we must accept that while the Cross of Jesus was a unique once-for-all event there is nonetheless a prolonged and *essential* sharing by God in human pain. This passionate engagement by God has an eternal quality that implies an extension of the passion of God into the very fabric of the human family. If the Cross is a symbol of the pain of God, the voice of this pain is the poor, oppressed and weak. In gospel terms this point is made most forcefully in the parable of the Last Judgement in the Gospel of Matthew (chapter 25). In the Cross, Father and Son both suffer in mutual surrender and from this surrender the Spirit is released as the power of God in the world that raises the poor and God-forsaken. All this contrasts with the power of the world, for the power of the crucified one is established in a moment of absolute self-abandonment.

The Cross of Christ undermines all attempts to spiritualise the meaning of salvation. The theology of the Cross is one of contradiction, conflict and non-conformity, as well as protest against all idolatry whether religious, social or political. Those who walk in the way of the Cross through lives of self-surrender become weak in the eyes of the world but capable of being freed and filled with a power the world does not possess. Faith is rooted in the paradox that God creates his liberation through those who recognise their own weakness. Liberation is, therefore, first of all being freed from the yoke of self-reliance. That is why the poor (who are radically powerless) are already the privileged of God and why they can evangelise the rich (self-sufficient). To know God means to abide with God in the Passion and so knowing God is related to our experience of evil in the world. Contemplation is not cosy isolation but is rooted in the engagement with this world that necessarily proceeds from a true following of the way of Christ. In the Cross, God takes on the pain of humanity and of our history. The paradox is that through involvement with the most negative side of human history, a death in failure, God opens up a new hope for the whole of history.

## 3. *Jesus' Cross is the consequence of his life*

A true following of Jesus and a true contemplation of God involves the Cross. This leads me to a final theme of contemporary theologies of the Cross: that the Passion is not the passive suffering of an uncomprehended fate. Rather, Christ's suffering arose from his actions, from his preaching of the nearness of the Kingdom, from his free attitude towards the Law and from his companionship with sinners.[11] Moltmann expresses this strongly: 'Jesus did not suffer passively from the world in which he lived but incited it against himself by his message and the life he lived.' So those who seek to follow Jesus cannot strictly be said to be imitators of his sufferings until and unless they accept his mission. Again Moltmann: 'He suffered on account of the liberating word of God and died on account of his liberating fellowship with those who were not free.' The Roman Catholic tradition would also add that it is possible to talk of the sufferings of ordinary life as 'crosses'. Certainly we need to be careful about this. It is easy to trivialise Calvary by identifying it with small setbacks. However, what this tradition emphasises positively is that, in baptism, we are united to Christ so closely that it is possible to talk of what we suffer as being 'in Christ'. Whatever we experience, even if trivial, *can* be made part of Jesus' redemptive mission which is continued in the Christian community, his Mystical Body. This is obviously not automatic. There has to be a real, personal desire to identify with Christ and his mission, otherwise little sufferings remain merely little sufferings. In human terms we can move beyond a fatalistic acceptance of suffering, small or great, to commit ourselves to the experience in a way that takes us out of ourselves. Apostolic suffering and death therefore mean a participation in Jesus' mission. The very idea of consciously following Jesus arises from a realisation of the profound conflict between Kingdom values and those of the world. The Cross cannot therefore leave us indifferent or detached; it demands commitment and engagement and 'taking sides'.

The Japanese theologian, Kosuke Koyama, also talks about this conflict in terms of a contrast of two 'powers'. Technological civilisation produces the spirit of 'efficiency' – this has what he calls 'Messiah-possibilities' because apparently it can *do* for us, and because it has tangible power. So the experience of salvation could become merely 'living in technological efficiency'. Koyama admits that efficiency is expressed as a positive value in, for example, the book of Genesis (1:28): 'And God blessed them, and God said to them, "Be fruitful and multiply and fill the earth and subdue it".' But it is also a temptation which results in a failure to hear the Word, because *the* Word takes the form of the Cross, of inefficiency. The wisdom of God, in purely human terms, is inefficient.[12]

The Cross is not arbitrary; rather it is the outcome of God's basic option in the Incarnation. The Cross is the vulnerability of God who chooses to become human in a world of conflict and sin. The Cross is the consequence of Jesus' life and chosen way, and so for a Christian a spirituality of the Passion cannot be reduced to pious meditation but consists in seeking to follow the way of Christ in our contemporary world and personal lives with all the consequences. So we are called, in the pattern of Jesus, to involve ourselves in a specific world and to take a stand against the sinfulness that gives that world its configuration. If we avoid even entering that process, then the Cross to which we offer our acceptance may not be the Cross of Jesus.

## The Cross and the Spiritual Exercises

I would now like to return to the specific spirituality of the Exercises and to suggest, briefly, ways in which this contemporary recovery of a theology of the Cross may enhance our understanding of St Ignatius's approach to Jesus' Passion. To an extent, the theme of the *vulnerable God who inevitably becomes the crucified God* is implicit throughout the Exercises from the moment that Ignatius invites us to contemplate the Incarnation. The option of God in Jesus for the world of humanity is made in the Incarnation and it is this option, to enter the powerlessness of the human condition, that is expressed in cumulative terms throughout the prayer of the next period of the Exercises which concentrates on contemplating the life and mission of the Jesus of history (the Second Week).

The self-emptying of God in Jesus is also implicitly expressed by Ignatius when he has Christ call those who seek to be his disciples 'to follow me in suffering' (Exx. 95) and when he describes the option for Christ as a way of poverty, contempt and humility (or in other words, self-giving or self-forgetfulness – Exx. 146). Thus when we reach the stage of explicitly contemplating Jesus' Passion it is the option of God for powerlessness that reaches its climax ('for example, it [the divinity] could destroy its enemies and does not do so' – Exx. 196) and it is a deepening awareness of a vulnerable God that will hopefully be one of the fruits of praying the Passion. In this prayer, the image of a vulnerable, self-forgetting God is highlighted when we contemplate the Cross which is Jesus' definitive movement out of himself, his moment of ultimate self-forgetfulness.

The 'movement-out-of-self', the 'being-totally-for-others' that is the very definition of God so beloved of theologians of the Cross is expressed, it seems to me, by Ignatius's continuous emphasis on Jesus' suffering being *for me*. God's option in Jesus is *for me*, for the world, not for suffering in itself. It is striking that people often seem to experience great dryness and absence of feelings when praying the Passion. When Ignatius, therefore, suggests in the Exercises that we ask for 'sorrow with Christ' when contemplating his Cross, it is not a question of pleasing emotion, cathartic tears, or a 'sorrow that makes me feel good'. Rather it will frequently be an experience of the desolation of Christ, the desolation of God.

Another theme of contemporary theologies of the Cross is that Jesus' Cross is not accidental or arbitrary but is *a consequence of his life and mission*. This accords very strikingly, it seems to me, with the way that the Passion in the Exercise finds its proper context in all that has gone before (especially in contemplating the human life of Jesus where we are already confronted with the radicality of Jesus' call to follow him). In the early part of the Exercises when we are invited to consider our lack of freedom or sin, the fundamental sin (the 'cosmic' sin of the angels in Ignatius's presentation) is described as 'pride' (Exx. 50). Clearly this pride is a profound contradiction of that freedom and self-forgetfulness which is the very nature of God and the way of the Cross – and thus the only way of responding to God in Jesus.

The decisive grounding for discipleship, or being with Christ in his ministry, lies in Ignatius's meditation on the 'Call of the King'. The call is precisely to 'follow me in suffering' (Exx. 95). The response is a prayer to 'imitate Christ in bearing all wrongs and all abuse and all poverty' (Exx. 98). This meditation appears at the very beginning of the contemplations on the life of Christ and so is the key to the subsequent prayer where Ignatius desires that the retreatant be saturated, as it were, with the attitude of Christ. Importantly, this 'saturation' is not merely a matter of emotional union. Closeness to Jesus is made explicit in discipleship. And this discipleship is expressed by a willingness to become profoundly committed to a concrete world – as Jesus was so engaged and committed. This inevitably involves conflict.[13] During the contemplation of the life and mission of Jesus (Second Week) the Cross is discovered to be central because necessarily involved in any call to discipleship. There is a kind of climax to this part of the Exercises in the desire 'to be received under His Standard', that is, the freedom to accept that suffering which is inevitably involved in following Jesus.

If we are to make this kind of response to Jesus' call, it is necessary that we 'take sides' and make options. This is affirmed very starkly in Ignatius's meditation entitled the 'Two Standards'. Such a choice is costly for from the very start it is the road to the Cross. The 'Two Standards' presents two modes of living: life seen in terms of pride, wealth and honour (or being by possessing) or in terms of the opposite – a freedom that enables us to live, to be, by giving ourselves in love. The choice is between two ways of working for the Kingdom of God. The question that is addressed to all of us is: Which kind of power really helps to usher in the Kingdom of God? Kosuke Koyama expresses this perceptively when he writes of life as a lunch-box or life as the Cross without a handle. The lunch-box is very neat and well-packaged and easy to carry. The Cross is angular, awkward and has no handle. Humanly speaking we prefer life to be like a lunch-box which we can carry for ourselves. For Christians, however, the call is accept the Cross which means 'life out of our hands'.[14] God's power is love and this is fleshed out in suffering and the Cross. In Ignatius's Exercises it is Satan who uses power to coerce – Christ merely gently invites. Dostoevsky's Grand Inquisitor in the *Brothers Karamazov* graphically illustrates, in his angry criticism of the returned and again imprisoned Christ, the very real temptation to opt for power as the 'sensible' way.

If our contemplation of the life and ministry of Jesus has really touched our depths we will inevitably be brought to a point of *krisis* or choice. Are we free enough, do we desire to make a fundamental option for Christ and his way of life? It is a decision, in the end, to be with Christ who triumphed through the Cross and restored the world to the Father only through the Cross. Once an initial option for Christ has been made it will, again inevitably, propel us forward to a sharing in the Cross of Christ in our own battle with the forces of evil as they work within our world. The point is that we are not called to choose the Cross or suffering in isolation or as good things in themselves but to *choose Jesus*. Thus praying the Passion in depth will merely make explicit the basic option for Christ.

In the Ignatian vision of praying the Passion the sorrow and compassion which we desire (Exx. 193) are not ends in themselves but rather to assist us 'not to be deaf to his [Christ's] call' (Exx. 91). The Cross is too concrete to stand for purely spiritualised values. We are truly to reject honour and turn our back on power except that of love. Jesus did not take on the Cross so as to shoulder the limitations of the human condition in some abstract sense. Rather he took on a conflict-ridden historical situation. Thus, with Jesus, we are also called to situate ourselves in a specific situation, a conflict-ridden world, as Jesus did.

Finally, a theme of contemporary theologies of the Cross is *a world in need of redemption*. The voice of the pain of God is the suffering of humanity and of human history. In the Cross, God takes on this pain. I have already suggested that contemplating the Passion focuses on Jesus' definitive movement out of himself, his definitive self-forgetfulness. To be drawn into the experience of the Passion will also be for us a process of moving out of self towards Jesus. But if the Jesus towards whom we move is he who, in the Cross, is most definitively the 'one for others', then our self-forgetfulness is *simultaneously* a movement to Christ in compassion and at the same time a sharing in his compassion for a broken humanity. Sharing in the suffering of Christ involves a participation in the *universal meaning* of his suffering.

If, as I have expressed, the Cross reveals that the true nature of God is to love totally, and if we are created in the image of this God, then the call to respond to this God in Jesus is a call to become truly ourselves in selfless love. Contemplating the Cross should create in us a growing willingness to 'die on a cross' for our fellows. Such contemplation will be a process of being freed from that centring on self which prevents us from loving as we desire and as the call of Christ demands. Individualism falsifies the contemplation of Jesus' death because it will turn us back onto ourselves, into self-conscious introspection, and thus contradict the movement out of self towards Christ who suffers in a continual conflict with the 'powers of darkness' in our world.

The Cross carries on it the full weight of human lack of freedom or sinfulness which issues in unmerited suffering, division and conflict, as well as the structures of injustice. The salvation that is effected by the Cross of Jesus is not merely a healing for individuals but it is also the ultimate destruction of the deadness at the heart of human history. In the Cross are broken down all the barriers created in our world by every kind of selfishness. On the Cross, Jesus becomes in himself 'the peace between us' (Eph. 2:14) creating a solidarity between all humans. In the light of the crucified Christ, who staked all the fullness of God for our salvation, we are also called to stand for creation against destruction, life not death, hospitality not hostility, mercy not cruelty. Justice, in the light of the Cross, is not just a political or sociological concept. It is part of that healing of the human condition that Jesus brings. For Jesus is the one who, in the words of the prophet Micah (6:8), did justice, loved kindly and walked humbly with his God.[15] At every moment we have to ask what kind of God the Cross reveals. Can a baby in a manger and a criminal on a cross speak of tyranny? Can such a God be understood in terms of retribution, punishment, fear, force and threat?

The Cross, as the ultimate expression of self-giving love, is the most profound critique of inquisition, racism, violent oppression and the prejudices of our culture. If we are able to see the Cross as representing and gathering into itself the countless crosses on which men and women continue to suffer in powerlessness, our entry into the mystery of Christ and his call will deepen immeasurably.

1. See St Ignatius Loyola, *The Spiritual Exercises*, ed. Louis J. Puhl, (Chicago 1951) – cited subsequently as Exx.
2. This point is made very strikingly in an article by Aloysius Pieris, 'Spirituality and Liberation' in *The Month* (April 1983), pp. 118–24.
3. See Jürgen Moltmann, *The Crucified God* (London 1984); and Jon Sobrino, *Christology at the Crossroads* (London 1978), especially ch. 6.
4. Sobrino, op.cit., pp. 182–201.
5. *Supra*, pp. 7–8. See also the article 'Spirituality', II G, by Josef Sudbrack in *Encyclopaedia of Theology*, ed. Karl Rahner (London 1975). I am also grateful to Dr Anne Murphy of Heythrop College London University, for letting me read the first chapter of her unpublished doctoral thesis.
6. See Jürgen Moltmann, *The Trinity and the Kingdom of God: the Doctrine of God* (London 1981); and *The von Balthasar Reader*, ed. M. Kehl, 27.
7. For example, G. Gutierrez, *A Theology of Liberation* (London 1974), and J. Segundo, *The Liberation of Theology* (London 1977).
8. For example, Moltmann, op.cit., ch. 6, and Sobrino, op.cit., pp. 217ff.
9. D. Bonhoeffer, *Letters and Papers from Prison* (London 1971), p. 300.
10. See Kenneth Leech, *True God* (London 1985), p. 300.
11. See especially, Sobrino, op.cit., pp. 201ff.
12. Kosuke Koyama, *Waterbuffalo Theology* (London 1974), ch. 5, *passim*.
13. See Sobrino, op.cit., appendix on 'The Christ of the Ignatian Exercises', especially pp. 407–12.
14. Kosuke Koyama, *No Handle on the Cross* (New York 1977).
15. Kosuke Koyama, *Mount Fuji and Mount Sinai* (London 1984), chapter 20, *passim*.

# 5
## Prayer and Images of God

---

While the search for holiness and the struggle at the heart
of discipleship, related to a renewed spirituality of the
Cross, are essential features of any Christian spirituality,
in practice it is prayer which is the element of Christian
life that raises most questions. Contemporary surveys of
religious belief and practice in the West seem to show that,
even among those who no longer claim membership of a
Church, prayer is still a common feature at times in their
lives. For the committed Christian, at the centre of faith is
a personal relationship with God and prayer expresses
this fact. It is the difference between treating Christianity
merely as an ethical code and taking seriously the presence
of the transcendent in the midst of experience.

The late Abraham Heschel, the American Jewish theologian, once commented that the central issue of prayer
was God. That is, that the important questions we ask or
the conclusions we draw about prayer cluster around the
'God question': what we say about God or God's relation
to human existence.[1] It might appear at first glance,
however, that for the average person the real problem
about prayer is the 'how'. It is certainly true that I suffered
for many years from a quite inadequate basic knowledge
about the rich variety of prayer-forms as well as from a
lack of guidance about growth in prayer and a lack of
encouragement in my search for an appropriate pattern of
prayer. We are so often trapped in the prayer of our youth
or even of our early childhood. I would maintain nonetheless, from some experience of trying to help others to grow
in prayer and from reflection on my own journey in prayer,
that far more basic than the problem of the 'how' of prayer
are our expectations. What do we expect of prayer and

why do we pray at all? What attitudes do we have either about the experiences we encounter in prayer or about having a relationship with God in general? It is not merely on the theoretical and theological level that I agree with Heschel's dictum but because of practical experience that the way we pray or what we think prayer *is* and therefore what we do about it manifest deeper attitudes about God, self and the world and about how these interconnect.

Perhaps my point is best illustrated by some examples of not uncommon images of God and the way they affect prayer which are admittedly rather crude but in which we can probably see something of ourselves. If God is seen as the possessor of immense power or as the top functionary then prayer becomes the way we apply to the highest authority to get things done. There are echoes here of 'It's not what you know but who you know . . .' We must persuade God to take our side and we must make sure that we keep God in the right mood. If God is seen as having some special kind of magic, then prayer is a useful way to unleash this magic in our favour at important moments – a very interventionist theory of God's way of responding to the human condition. Perhaps, on the contrary, God is actually rather weak and open to flattery or bribery and so prayer then becomes a way of saying, 'If you will do this for me, I will do that for you'. Sometimes prayer works on the bureaucratic model: God, not satisfied with one form or one prayer, demands, as any self-respecting lower-grade public official might, that everything be filled out in triplicate. Prayer here works through quantity although we may occasionally be slightly discomforted by those words of Jesus, 'In your prayers do not babble as the pagans do, for they think that by using many words they will make themselves heard' (Matt. 6:7).

There is always that nagging question (beloved not merely of philosophers of religion but also of the average praying person), 'Does God intervene to change the way things normally are?' We pray for good weather for the annual parish garden party or the village cricket match or we pray that we pass those examinations even though we have not really done sufficient revision. Again, there is prayer as a 'last resort' when we have tried everything else;

when things are clearly hopeless we are invited to turn to God in prayer. The court of final appeal. Many of us, whatever we say in theory, see God as arbitrary and life as too unpredictable. And so prayer can become a way of helping God to get the 'divine act in order' – a kind of nudge in the celestial ribs as a reminder that there are other interested parties in the universe. For many people God is a rather Olympian figure (far away and quite beyond our understanding) and prayer often takes the form of propitiation, of keeping God happy and at a safe distance in order to minimise the possible damage. I will only approach God with any seriousness when I absolutely have to. Somehow all these ways of thinking have something to do with seeing God essentially as *power* and *distant*.

To be fair, of course, I should also add that not all images of God are discomforting. There are also a range of 'domesticated' Gods going the rounds. The Russian Orthodox Metropolitan Anthony of Sourozh, whose books on prayer have proved very popular, once said in an interview that he found that for the English (I am sure this is not limited to the English however) religion tended to be rather safe. He suggested that to enter into the presence of God is to be in the cave of a tiger; the experience was ultimately uncontrollable. Too often we turn God into a domesticated pussy-cat. If I may pursue the image, God as a cat fits into our laps quite snugly, the experience is cosy and stroking the cat and hearing it purr gives us a pleasant sensation. God, however, is no pussy-cat and prayer is not a matter of stroking God in order to get good feelings![2]

Our image of God, the kind of God we believe in, is to my mind crucial to the way our journey of prayer proceeds. Is our God essentially engaged with human experience or disengaged? Is our God primarily judge or saviour? Do we treat God as ruler or lover? Does God communicate, offer hope and mercy? Is God faithful and is God interested in our world? In his book, *The Social God*, Kenneth Leech writes about the continued presence of some classical Christian heresies about God.[3] If we reflect upon these we can see their implications for the way we pray. The Monophysite God is distant and did not truly become one of us, for Christ was only God under the *appearances* of human nature. There is, therefore, no redemption for the human situation. If this is so a dichotomy opens up between prayer and everyday experience. The problems of life are, in the context of prayer, merely a distraction. My ordinary experience is not really valuable or spiritual. The Gnostic God is even more common these days. The key to everything is 'special knowledge', for God is only available to the initiates. Once again the material world is irrelevant and only truly spiritual activities are important. I cannot help feeling that this God is present in *certain* aspects of some contemporary schools of meditation and even in the less critical circles within the charismatic renewal. Gnostic prayer and spirituality is self-centred and presents peace, stillness and tranquillity as ends in themselves. The method is the meaning. Because religious experience is limited to purely 'spiritual activities', such a spirituality will be culturally conformist rather than critical or prophetic.

The Marcionite God originally involved ditching the Old Testament images entirely. Here the belief that God is merely love and life is all joy is the abiding weakness. Jesus would not say 'boo to a goose' let alone to a Pharisee. Because such a theology tends to reject the reality of the sufferings of Christ, there is really no meaning in human suffering in general. The spirituality that arises from this will tend to have a difficulty with experiencing the reality of God in our ambiguity, our mess, our sin. There is a lack of freedom where we cannot admit that prayer is not all joy. The Arian God is essentially distant and despotic. There can be no real communication with this God and certainly no personal relationship. This God's action is frequently arbitrary and so I experience God as, more often than not, one who gets in the way of what I desire or find attractive. There is often much Arian 'theology' in the spirituality of those who view prayer as a duty. God is mainly not there.

At this point you may feel that I have been very one-sided – that the images of God that I have described are all very inadequate and in many cases thoroughly negative. My defence is simply that I believe that inadequate images of God are far more common than we sometimes believe and that this provides one of the most effective obstacles to growth and to the healing of that disharmony at the centre of each which stands in the way of a movement to spiritual freedom.

Everyone comes to prayer with certain images of God that are operative in his or her life. There is a sense in which none of these *can* be perfectly correct. Clearly God is always beyond our capacity to define, to control or have within our grasp by capturing in a single image. Every individual human image of God is necessarily one-sided. Even if we took all the images of God from the Christian tradition and our own experience, the reality of God would be still greater than the sum of the whole. Yet images are neither invalid nor useless. We all have them and we all need them as we seek to order our experience. Some are more helpful and creative and others less so or even fundamentally destructive. The destructive may be more obviously negative – such as one of God as a celestial policeman. However, some apparently benign images (such as a God who never challenges, who never makes me feel anything other than joy) can also be real barriers in the way of growth. In embarking on the journey of prayer we will find that, for all of us, there will be a refinement of images, for to cling exclusively to any of them would be idolatry and would constitute a blockage to further movement. However, what of those of us who have images of God that are essentially negative or dangerously destructive? They too are blocked for, with such images of God, they lack the firm ground from which to view the negative side of their lives and experience. With such images we cannot really afford to have God show us our true selves, especially our sinfulness or need for growth and healing for to admit to sin or failure without knowing the ever-present healing mercy of God is to enter into a black prison with no discernible exit. And yet without such a realisation there is no possibility of responding to a God who calls only those who are needy and are prepared to admit it.

At the beginning of the *Spiritual Exercises* of St Ignatius of Loyola there is a passage entitled the 'Principle and

Foundation'.[4] The rather antiquated statements, couched in the language of scholastic theology, concerning our relationship with God, self and the world, may lead the casual reader to underestimate their importance. It seems clear, however, that St Ignatius here summarised the dispositions needed to proceed further on the spiritual journey. Ignatius's own experience was that no real progress was possible unless a person was securely grounded in a realisation of God's creative love. The only way that we can appropriate this is by faith through placing ourselves in God's hands and progressing in what Ignatius calls 'interior knowledge'. In his introductory remarks to the *Spiritual Exercises* he says: 'Let the Creator deal immediately with the creature and the creature with his Creator and Lord.'[5] It is not 'much knowledge that fills and satisfies the soul, but the intimate understanding and relish of the truth'.[6] This idea of 'relish' underlines the difference between a purely intellectual belief in the goodness and creativity of God and an affective experience of God as one who accepts us as we are. The 'Principle and Foundation', therefore, grounds the whole dynamic of the Exercises in a biblical faith – that all reality is, by its very existence, within God's active and creative love. In a wider context of prayer the movement towards inward freedom begins from a deep realisation, albeit imperfect, that God is faithful and trustworthy.

The journey of prayer, therefore, involves a necessary process of being touched by God's personal love in creation. We are called to be open to God in order to be filled. If I am convinced of God's unending fidelity I can be drawn to seek that spiritual freedom which will enable me to surrender all my desires to God's call and to 'praise, reverence and serve him' (the words of the Principle and Foundation) in every moment and experience. We must begin with the *reality* of God – not merely that God exists but exists *for me*. Truly to 'praise, reverence and serve' God implies a mutuality of love. In order to respond in this way I need to become more free and able to be open to the ways in which God wishes to communicate love to me rather than the ways I think that I ought to be loved. But I cannot make myself free from my dependencies and fears on my own. Awareness of God's love and faithfulness precedes response just as the father's love was already active in the pigsty drawing the Prodigal Son home (Luke 15:11–32). Without this awareness our own personal pigsty, for all its darkness and dirt, may seem far more secure than the world outside. We cannot leave behind our false securities unless we are first drawn more and more towards something, someone else. In my own life, I am most aware of becoming free through the gift of human relationships – of being loved and accepted and thus discovering my own value. The sense of a 'hole' in my life which needs to be filled with less constructive things decreases in proportion. God leads us to freedom by showing the reality and security of divine love to us. Hence the importance of that 'interior knowledge' of the truth of which St Ignatius wrote. We come to love and to trust only the people we know. True love, founded on true knowledge, enables us to allow the other to be himself or herself. And we have to let God be God; to let the Spirit expose our idols.

It is sometimes the case that the idea of praising, reverencing and serving God seems to point towards an ideal of duty however painful. Is it that God is so vain that people are created merely to offer praise? Thus such language can reinforce doubtful images of God. We need to realise that God creates in order to share infinite love and that true 'praise, reverence and service' of God is based on the principle of attraction not imposition. If we succeed in catching a glimpse of the real God we cannot help but praise. Praise can only be the action of a free person, and in this free act that expresses total dependence we do not become less than human. Indeed, as we come to realise slowly, it is only in this kind of dependence that we become fully ourselves.

## Images true and false

Real problems arise in our spiritual journey if we have some thoroughly bad images of God that are strongly operative in our lives. When a person is not able to allow God to influence deep interior feelings, indeed cannot afford to allow such feelings to surface, it is often because of false images. These will usually be negative: God as tyrant, manipulator, puppet-master, judge or false friend. Such images will strongly influence the way we listen to or avoid God's word. Yet they are often quite difficult to diagnose particularly if they are buried deeply within us. Very often such images go back to events in our lives which still need to be fully faced, accepted and healed. I remember one woman who deeply resented her father's profound puritanism. So many crucial decisions in the early part of her life had been overshadowed by her father's narrowness and interference. This, she felt, had led to an unsatisfactory career choice and to her remaining a spinster. Consequently her ability to relate to any idea of God as 'Father' was greatly complicated. It is, in my experience, so often the case that our relationship with God is determined by our experience of human relationships. But we must be careful not to assume that all stunted affectivity in prayer is rooted in negative experiences of life. Sometimes there is a false image of prayer itself – for example that feelings do not count and should be ignored.

It is sometimes helpful to monitor or keep in touch with our reactions to common images of God in Scripture. How are we affected by a particular image – does it bring fear or peace? Feelings of discomfort need to be acknowledged and then expressed freely to God in prayer. But for this to be possible, of course, we have to be clear that there are no inappropriate feelings in prayer. We need to be convinced that God can and does meet us where we are, is infinitely patient and waits for us. This belief may itself be reinforced by using for prayer scripture passages that speak of God's faithfulness and accepting love, such as the psalms or passages from Isaiah. What words, phrases or images most strike me? I can remain with them, repeat them or merely focus on them and allow their positive power to go deeper until they fill my consciousness. Healing and forgiveness stories from the gospels are also often appropriate. The use of imagination, which I shall discuss later, may prove a helpful approach here. Afterwards it is helpful to reflect on reactions and feelings. What gave me peace? What disturbed me? And what does this tell me about the gifts God seeks to give me at this moment?

In the end it is vital to reach the point of feeling that there is nothing that we need to hide in God's presence. When this is the case we can ask God to give light and ultimately to change images which are blocks to a more intimate relationship. Sometimes we have to stay at this point for a long time and the process of healing may be slow and imperceptible. Or the breakthrough may be sudden and dramatic. One man whom I met on a retreat had a considerable range of negative images of God (to the point where he really hated God) and after some days felt that there was no point in going on. By bedtime this mood was so strong that he could not sleep and finally after some hours of struggle he ceased to fight and, as it were, said 'Who are you, God?' In a way that is difficult to describe God was able to get through and to be revealed for the first time as someone who did not threaten but could heal. The man did not leave, and over the remaining days was able to pray with great peace. By the end of the retreat he was able to say 'Yes' to the reality of a loving God in areas of his life that had seemed, up to that point, quite barren and destructive.

Frequently we have problems with the 'will of God'. 'Thy will be done' slips easily from the lips but fails to engage with our inner being. The sense that God's will is unknowable is frequently associated less with intellectual difficulties than with a lack of inner freedom. To 'know' the will of God at the deepest level is to realise that this will and my best interests truly intersect. Without this realisation it is easy to blame God for our mistakes and bad choices. God seems to block every promising avenue in life. God asks too much – God is arbitrary. How many of us, I wonder, have been tempted to take the side of the young man who approaches Jesus to ask what more he must do to inherit eternal life? 'He's a good, sincere person. Why do you ask the impossible?' The will of God seems to be a kind of heavenly version of the great disembodied foot that crushed unsuspecting people in the satirical British television series 'Monty Python'.

Often our problems with God's will are associated less

with the past than with fears about the future. The idea that I am being called to take on Christ's yoke may seem an unmanageable burden despite disclaimers that it is in fact easy and light. I cannot afford to get too close because 'you never know what God is going to ask of you'. We compensate by a kind of stubborn cheerfulness. Prayer is always a 'beautiful experience' without challenge because we cannot afford to let it be anything else. God's will is an eternal blueprint, already packaged and quite extrinsic to our desires. It is vital for us to get in touch with this attitude and to enable God to show us that we can allow ourselves to let go. For unless we come to *desire* God's will in our very roots (and not merely accept it reluctantly) we cannot be wholehearted in our prayer or actions. Maybe we need to hear once again the invitation to make our desires explicit in the words of Jesus to John the Baptist's disciples: 'What do you seek . . . what are you looking for?' (John 1:35–9). What are *my* desires?

There are other less radically damaging images which are nonetheless important in our life of prayer. For example, it may be that I seek to be God and so implicitly refuse creaturehood in many areas of my life. Or I may lack sufficient gratitude for God's gifts. On the other hand there may be a degree of self-doubt which needs to be touched by an awareness of God's kindness. 'Yet even if these forget, I will never forget you. See, I have branded you on the palms of my hands . . .' (Isa. 49:14–16). I can accept myself as lovable and become ever more aware that even if nobody else were to love me, God certainly would. Perhaps, again, my God is too pure. This God cannot possibly be involved with a person like me, or be found in this place or situation. Many of us feel that God is elusive – that it is we who have to do all the chasing. These feelings can be eroded by praying with such scripture passages as Psalm 139 in which God continually searches for us down the corridors of our lives, or the parable of the shepherd who seeks out the one sheep (Luke 15:4–7), or the husband in the prophecy of Hosea who seeks out the unfaithful wife to bring her home, or perhaps the risen Christ who penetrates the fearful defences of the apostles in the upper room (John 20).

In the context of inadequate images I would also suggest that for many of us there is still a narrowness and imbalance in our images of God in that they are rooted exclusively in male language. The feminine aspect of God has not played a significant role in Christian spirituality until fairly recently. True, feminine imagery was used by some Syriac writers in the early Christian centuries and there are other examples among medieval Cistercians and mystics (Julian of Norwich being perhaps the best known example). However this emphasis did not enter the mainstream of popular spirituality. Because our images of God are closely associated with the way we understand discipleship, prayer and our ways of relating to people, events and the whole created world, it must be true that we have lost a great deal by an exclusive emphasis on male imagery. My own perceptions have certainly been challenged and have begun to alter and be enriched by reading and hearing first-hand about religious experiences where female images of God have played a significant role. I have to admit, however, that my inherited and one-sided images are deeply ingrained and so, in my own inner experiences, both the feminine in God and its implications for my ways of seeing and relating still impinge only occasionally.

For those of us who pray with Scripture and perhaps, from time to time, use imagination to enter into the meaning of gospel passages, it is worth noting that while not all images that emerge offer us the truth about God they may nevertheless lead to a fuller understanding of ourselves because they are projections of our own limitations, fears or ambiguous feelings. One man imagined Jesus meeting him on the road and saying: 'I'm not going to love you until you love me better.' When this happens we can afterwards reflect and ask ourselves what the experience did for us – what feelings were present. I have found that aspects of St Ignatius's 'Rules for discernment' in the *Spiritual Exercises* may then be helpful. What an image does to us is an indication of where it comes from: 'Then it is characteristic of the evil spirit to harass with anxiety, to afflict with sadness, to raise obstacles backed by fallacious reasonings that disturb the soul.'[7] The main point therefore, is that all images have value and may teach us something illuminating even if, initially, they seem rather confusing.

To speak more positively, my feeling is that one of the most basic images for growth that we need to appropriate is that of God as loving creator. In prayer, something like Isaiah, chapter 43 (verses 1–7) can often be a great help for those of us who sometimes feel nervous about the effect of God's power in our lives. To acknowledge God as creator is also to realise God's merciful care: 'Fear not, I have redeemed you.' Here we can begin to appreciate that the call to become human, to take on an identity, precedes anything else that God asks. 'I have called you by your name . . .' Prayer is frequently a slow process of knowing and accepting myself and so to be capable of healthy relationships with others and of accepting responsibility. The scriptural image of God as creator may also help us to understand that God creates by self-giving: 'I have called you by *my* name . . .' A very common experience in prayer is to realise slowly that I cannot think of God in terms of human limitations: 'My ways are not your ways' (Isa. 55:7–9). In using scriptural images from the Old Testament it is also helpful to know that for the people of Israel the idea that God was creator was also an assurance of divine generosity; that the faithfulness experienced in the past was a guarantee of God's fidelity in the future (for example, Isa. 49:14–15; 54:6). We shall also have to come to terms with the fact that God's fidelity does not guarantee an absence of disturbance in our lives. Such is not the peace that God gives. God is not an over-indulgent 'daddy' or 'mummy'. To pass through fire and water reminds us that to be human is a risky business (Isa. 43:2) but to accept these risks is to put one's trust in God's promise: 'I will be with you'.

We need to be aware that for those of us for whom God's presence has always been an underlying reality it is difficult to get inside the skin of people for whom it is a more uncertain business. Like most Christians, I suppose, I have had doubts from time to time in my life about aspects of Christian belief. At other times the presence of God has not been particularly tangible – I have experienced dryness and a feeling of distance. I certainly accepted that doubts were part of the human experience of faith. However, in the last analysis I was always sure that there was God who was real and active in my life even if I could not fully grasp this reality or 'feel' it intensely. Not so long ago I had a quite new experience. A virus infection that would not go away led to a short course of drugs which had the unfortunate side-effect of temporary depression. Part of this experience was to sense briefly but very intensely the absence of God, to feel in reality what life without a God was like. Such an experience inevitably changes a number of things. For one thing, I had to come to terms with the fact that I had, to an extent, taken God for granted and God's presence as well. You might say that I learned something more about the freedom of God as well as about myself in that experience. My image of God was subtly altered.

Progress, as I suggested earlier, involves being able to look with increasing honesty at our limitations, failures and sinfulness. But before we can even begin to do this in a healthy and helpful way we must possess at least a basic trust in and some personal experience of God's sustaining love. Otherwise an awareness of sin remains merely an unhealthy introspection or self-centred guilt. We must be patient with ourselves in order to let this awareness, this safe ground, emerge in the healing love of God. This takes time and we need not despair because we do not seem to get things right all at once. Many of us have a problem with perfection: a list of 'oughts' that, hard as we try and unreasonable as they seem, it is difficult to ignore. This may sometimes make it extremely hard to accept that our experiences of the moment, which are always imperfect and incomplete, are nevertheless authentic. 'I ought to be doing better; I should be able to succeed; I can surely pray better than this; God has given me so many chances to overcome my weakness which I have failed to use.' Maybe at times we will be resentful at our limitations, at not being in total control, or angry at the vagaries of life. When this is the case we should not be afraid to express these honest feelings and reactions and to ask God to give that inner enlightenment which is necessary before we can finally let God be God.

Our understanding of God is clearly at the centre of the

question: 'What is prayer?' and so it seemed appropriate to reflect on this before everything else. However, we have also inherited an understanding of prayer as a structured activity, distinct from the normal pattern of everyday life, that demands extended periods of time. If our images of God are sometimes a problem, this second factor is hardly less so. We have been inadequately exposed to other elements of the Christian tradition of prayer that affirm the possibility of turning all activity into a 'spiritual exercise' and of finding God in all things. This is the issue to which I want to turn my attention.

1. Abraham J. Heschel, *Man's Quest for God* (New York 1954), p. 87.
2. Metropolitan Anthony, *School of Prayer* (London 1970), Introduction, pp. xv-xvi.
3. Kenneth Leech, *The Social God* (London 1981), pp. 30–4.
4. St Ignatius Loyola, *The Spiritual Exercises*, ed. Louis J. Puhl (Chicago 1951) – subsequently cited as Exx. 'The Principle and Foundation' is Exx. 23.
5. Exx. 15.
6. Exx. 2.
7. 'Rules for the discernment of spirits', Exx. 315.

# 6
## Time and Times for Prayer

One of the most common problems that people mention in conversations about prayer is that of 'time'. This may manifest itself as an inability to find sufficient space for extended prayer, a lack of energy, little or no solitude even when there is time, and perhaps a feeling that prayer does not engage easily with the rest of life. 'Time' is a problem, in other words, when it implies a daily or at least a regular extended experience of structured and formal prayer in 'periods' distinct from all other activities. A mother with two young children and a husband who worked mainly at home once described to me her frustration at not being able to find more than the odd moment alone for prayer. In desperation she retired to the bathroom and locked herself inside, but even there she was likely to be interrupted after a few minutes by a young child enquiring whether anything was the matter. There was not merely very little time alone but no guarantee that what solitude there was would not be invaded.

Anyone involved pastorally with people must wonder how to respond to this and a myriad other tales. What general approach to prayer is, in fact, reinforced in people when they ask advice about it? I remember that, as students, a group of us were surprised by remarks passed by a priest who had the reputation for being an excellent spiritual director. Was it necessarily the case, he asked, that a formal, structured approach to prayer was suited to everyone? Our assumption, I suppose, was that not to pray in this way was to 'fail' and to 'lose touch' with *real* prayer. We had been warned as Jesuit novices that the discipline of daily meditation would be hard in a working life but the implication was that to let go of it was the beginning of a serious decline.

No doubt most of us are sympathetic to friends who mention problems about 'time' and 'times' in their life of prayer, but are we always realistic in our response? I cannot help feeling that the structured, formal model of prayer is still frequently presented, from the best of motives, as some kind of universal ideal. I do not suppose that most people who describe genuine and unavoidable difficulties are simply exhorted to greater effort – although it is unfortunate that some writing on prayer and on spiritual direction still seems to imply that such problems are largely of a person's own making. In the main, the way any of us talk with others about prayer is governed by whether we have experienced similar struggles and by whether we have ourselves moved beyond a one-dimensional understanding of prayer. It is, for example, sometimes difficult for members of religious communities to break away from a 'monastic' model of the Christian life – certainly the celibate has little experience of the day-to-day pressures of family life and a house full of children. In some books on prayer the degree to which we 'give time' is linked to the depth of our 'desire for God' without much qualification. It is disturbing when a still popular reference work known to many Christians (*The New Catholic Encyclopaedia*) can talk about how often we pray in terms of obligation (in the article on 'Prayer, theology of') and suggest that to omit prayer for a month or two could be a mortal sin. The writer concludes that 'the good Christian will pray many times each day'.

## Theological assumptions

Part of our problem is, of course, the range of theological presuppositions that, explicitly or implicitly, underlie our understanding of prayer. A number of contemporary writers have rightly suggested that questions about prayer really cluster around the 'God question'.[1] Once again the important question is: What image of God is operative? Is our God distant and uninvolved, and is our prayer as a consequence less a relationship than an effort to gain God's power for ourselves, to get it under control, to make God sit up and take notice? I have already suggested that much inadequate spirituality (and not least theories of prayer) results from those attempts to 'reinterpret' God that lose touch with the traditional doctrines of Trinity and Incarnation and which thereby upset that delicate balance of the transcendence-immanence of God which governs the way we understand and respond to life and the world. Our understanding of God necessarily involves God's relationship with human experience and with the material world. Does God offer love as a free gift or has it to be earned? Is prayer essentially God's action or is it our effort expressed by quantity? Is the material world a snare and a delusion and the search for holiness a flight from the world? Or are prayer and life intimately linked so that it can be said that the aim of prayer is ultimately the deepening awareness of God as 'all in all' leading to a greater engagement with the world of everyday events? The answers to such questions will govern our attitude to the 'how' of prayer.

*Prayer in Christian tradition*

The understanding of prayer that places great emphasis on solitude, withdrawal, formal structures and extended time represents only one strand in the Christian tradition. Alternative approaches emphasise, in different ways, turning *all* action into work for God. 'I look for God in all things and try to please him in everything I do.'[2] Theologically this means taking the consequences of the Incarnation seriously – that we cannot speak of specifically 'spiritual' areas of life or 'spiritual activities', for no aspect of human life is outside the love and activity of God. We live in a graced world and materiality is 'full of grace'.

While teaching about personal prayer has always given some attention to method, it seems fair to say that the emphasis on formalised prayer time begins to predominate with the development of structured meditation in the later Middle Ages. Prior to this development, prayer tended to be rather informal. Thus the prayer of the desert fathers was simple, silent and brief. Cassian, the most systematic of the desert teachers recommended brief and frequent prayer. The way to make prayer 'unceasing' throughout the day was to take short scripture verses that could be recollected constantly.

> This you should write on the threshold and door of your mouth, this you should place on the walls of your house and in the recesses of your heart, so that when you fall on your knees in prayer this may be your chant as you kneel, and when you rise up from it to go forth to all the necessary business of life it may be your constant prayer as you stand.[3]

Constant prayer is emphasised by other desert teachers such as Lucius who opposed those who sought to suppress work in favour of lengthy formal prayer:

> I will show you how, while doing my manual work, I pray without interruption. I sit down with God, soaking my reeds and plaiting my ropes, and I say, 'God have mercy on me; according to your great goodness and according to the multitude of your mercies save me from my sins'. So he asked them if this were not prayer and they replied it was.[4]

For Lucius, a life orientated towards God was itself prayer. This was also underlined in the West by the Rule of St Benedict (chapter 20) which emphasised that we are heard by God not because of the length of our prayer but because of purity of heart: 'Therefore prayer should be short and pure,' as a general rule. Extending this teaching beyond the monastery to the lives of ordinary Christians, St Augustine left an important treatise on prayer dedicated to Proba, a widow, and meant for domestic use by herself and her friends. Long prayer is acceptable if there is time, but we do not *need* this. Consequently Augustine approves of the practice of the desert fathers and their use of 'very brief, quickly dispatched prayers' (*orationes brevissimas et raptim quodammodo jaculatas*).[5]

In the West, meditation remained essentially free in form up to about the eleventh century and was closely linked to the prayerful rumination of Scripture known as *lectio divina*. This way of praying was not regulated by a fixed timetable nor cultivated by any formalised method. It was essentially a free activity and probably involved the recall and 'ejaculation' of phrases throughout the day.

Methods of prayer as we understand them probably took root about the twelfth century (for example Hugh of St Victor and Guigues du Pont) and were intended to organise meditation in order to make it easier. A clear distinction began to be made between the different phases of *lectio divina*. The great period of development of formal meditation began in the fourteenth century in the context of a movement known as the *devotio moderna* in Germany and the Low Countries. Gerard Groote composed a systematic treatise on 'the four kinds of things to be meditated'. Other representatives of the *devotio moderna* – such as Florent Radewijns, Gerard of Zutphen and Jan Mombaer – further developed the art of meditation, arranging it in groups of exercises day by day, week by week and month by month. This tradition of systematic meditation gave birth to a vast literature over the next two centuries including works by St Ignatius of Loyola, St Francis de Sales, Dom Augustine Baker and some seventeenth-century Anglican divines.

Yet the tradition that prayer need not involve extended time nor structured method remained alive. Even the great contemplative Carmelites stressed the unity of prayer and action. St Teresa of Avila could happily say that 'the Lord is among the saucepans':

> If contemplation, mental and vocal prayer, nursing the sick, the work of the house and the most menial labour all serve this guest who comes to eat and drink and converse with us, why should we choose to minister to him in one way rather than another?[6]

Although St Ignatius of Loyola is frequently portrayed as methodical about prayer this is really limited to the particular context of the Spiritual Exercises. In general, St Ignatius reacted against an over-formalised approach. His emphasis was not so much on withdrawal as on responding to God's presence and action in life. His comments on prayer in his letters and in the *Constitutions* of the Jesuits recognised that a full life did not leave much free time. In many ways the teaching of St Ignatius offers one of the clearest approaches to the problems both of time for prayer and of the link between prayer and the remainder of life. I shall develop this later.

Within a short time of the founder's death, the Society of Jesus succumbed to a suspicion of contemplative and free-wheeling prayer. This was partly due to a fear of the heresy of 'illuminism' and was partly a reaction against the excessively contemplative approach of some Spanish Jesuits. It is not unfair to say that this process had a profound effect on the wider Church. The growing emphasis on structured meditation necessarily involved an awareness of time to a much greater degree than more free and affective prayer.[7]

Even this very selective glance at the history of Christian prayer reveals a tradition that is much wider than the understanding inherited as a result of the process of formalisation. A number of emphases seem particularly relevant to our problem of 'time' and 'times'. For example, it is possible to turn all activity into a work for God and it is possible to conceive of prayer as unceasing. I would now like to focus on some particular expressions of this approach in a little more detail.

## St Ignatius and contemplation in action

St Ignatius of Loyola saw God as dwelling in all things and 'labouring' for people in the world and experiences of life. This understanding is present especially in the 'Contemplation to attain the love of God' in the Exercises – which is arguably both a method of prayer and a way of understanding the process of prayer in daily life.[8] It points to an awareness of God in all times and in all things so that contemplation and action become not two distinct things but inextricably linked one to another.

Even within the formal experience of the Exercises, St Ignatius in a sense demythologises the 'magic' of prayer-times as the only context for the action of the Spirit by emphasising the need for a much wider context of aware-ness and reflection (Exx. 73–4 and the different approaches to the 'Examen of consciousness', Exx. 24–43). In everyday life it is said that St Ignatius did not ask how long a person contemplated but how often he made the Examen. Our understanding of this process has sometimes been limited to an examination of failings but it really involves the cultivation of a general awareness of God's action and presence in daily life. We are invited to ask the Spirit to show us where to be thankful, where God has sought to communicate during the day in ordinary and even trivial events and, looking ahead, where we most need guidance and grace for the following day. This process of finding God in more and more of life was, in the mind of St Ignatius, vital for people whose activities prevented them from indulging in lengthy periods of prayer. In practice, for many people the 'Examen of consciousness' (as it is known today in preference to the narrower 'of conscience'), or regular contemplative reflection on the experiences of everyday life, may be the only *regular* prayer they are able to manage in a busy life.[9]

Apart from its emphasis on awareness of God in ordinary events, the Examen also involves a degree of self-awareness, of how I am responding or failing to respond (where I need conversion, repentance or sorrow) to the promptings of the Spirit in and through the demands of daily life. In other words it may become a helpful context for growth in an attitude that St Ignatius saw as vital – what he called 'self-abnegation' or forgetfulness of self. Nowadays this may appear a rather off-putting phrase. However, in essence, it describes a movement away from self-centredness to self-giving and generosity to God and fellow humans. In the Exercises it is generosity rather than simply time given to prayer that is so important. Da Camara, the compiler of St Ignatius's autobiography, reported that St Ignatius put more emphasis on self-denial than on length of prayer. It has been suggested that 'self-abnegation' was St Ignatius's test of authenticity both of action and prayer because each of these can be vitiated by self-seeking. If there is genuine self-sacrifice in ordinary activities it does not take long to find God.[10]

Maurice Giuliani, a contemporary expert on giving the Spiritual Exercises 'in daily life' (that is, without withdrawal to a retreat centre), points out that for St Ignatius, an 'exercise' was *any* action that prepared a person to receive the grace of God. Outside a closed retreat this will not be limited to times of formal prayer. Indeed he is dubious about reinforcing the special status of formal prayer 'as if it offered a privileged context for the most intense spiritual experiences'.[11] The 'attentiveness to God' that is fundamental to the Exercises is not confined to formal prayer. Indeed, Giuliani argues, part of the aim of the Exercises 'in daily life' and, one might argue, of Ignatian spirituality as a whole, is precisely to transform ordinary activities into 'spiritual exercises' so that a person may come to see that each day is rich in moments when it is possible to experience God as present in the most ordinary of human activities and in our everyday relationships.

It is not, of course, that all human activities are automatically explicit 'spiritual exercises' – this depends on a context of reflection (perhaps through the Examen) and a growth in selflessness. Thus, in his letters, St Ignatius emphasises that it is the giving of time to other activities precisely 'for God's service' that makes this truly continuous prayer.[12] Those who resent the distraction of activity may, if they accept this 'for God's service', make it the 'equivalent of the union and recollection of uninterrupted contemplation'.[13] In a letter to Francis Borgia, St Ignatius suggests quite clearly that length of time does not necessarily mean real prayer. He speaks with approval of the tradition of the desert fathers concerning brief prayer and of St Augustine's letter to Proba (already quoted) on the value of ejaculatory prayer throughout an active day.[14]

Perhaps the breadth of St Ignatius's understanding of prayer is best summarised in a letter to Father Brandao concerning young Jesuits who were busy with studies. They should:

... seek God's presence in all things, in their conversations, their walks, in all they see, taste, hear, understand, in all their actions, since his divine Majesty is truly in all things by his presence, power and essence ... But this method is an excellent exercise to prepare for great visitations of Our Lord even in prayers that are rather short.[15]

*The sacrament of the present moment*

St Ignatius's teaching might be described in terms of the sacramental quality of all time and all activities. Two other spiritual writers are regaining a contemporary popularity precisely because they take up the same theme and offer a spirituality suited to people with little time for extended prayer. Jean-Pierre de Caussade (1675–1751) was himself a Jesuit whose conferences and letters were edited in the nineteenth century into a volume that became known as *Abandonment to Divine Providence*. De Caussade emphasised that perfection was not so much to do with exceptional 'states' as with self-giving to God's will in whatever situation we live and work. God is present in everything, clearly or obscurely, in the guise of something we can do, bear or enjoy. Each passing moment is a 'veil of God' which if scrutinised and interpreted by faith becomes an unveiling of God. He actually uses the term 'the sacrament of the present moment' to describe this possibility. De Caussade points clearly to the necessity of integrating the spiritual with daily life, thereby transforming it into a state of prayer.

The seventeenth-century Carmelite, Brother Lawrence, in *The Practice of the Presence of God*, refuses to distinguish between times of prayer and all other times which we can transform into 'spiritual exercises' by doing for God what we would otherwise do simply for ourselves. Again, as with St Ignatius, the crucial thing is to purge our actions of selfishness:

> He found the best means of drawing near to God was through the common tasks which obedience laid down for him, purging them as far as lies in us from every human ingredient and performing them all for the pure love of God.

> It was, he said, enormous self-deception to believe that the time of prayer must be different from any other. We are equally bound to be one with God by what we do in times of action as by the time of prayer at its special hour. His prayer was simply the presence of God, his soul unconscious to all else but love.[16]

Many contemporary Christians find the writings of de Caussade and Brother Lawrence (both available in popular editions) attractive not because they provide a quantifiable *method* of prayer but because they affirm what many of us already experience: that an awareness of God in everyday life and an offering of our ordinary activities to God is possible, helpful and authentic prayer.

*Mindfulness*

While there are obvious dangers in a naive comparison of Christian and non-Christian meditation and experience, certain elements of the Buddhist 'way of mindfulness' seem to complement the teachings of de Caussade and Brother Lawrence. This is especially the case with the extension of a meditative attitude beyond concentrated moments into the activities of normal life, and also with the importance of eliminating selfishness. Rather than 'being present' only partially to our ordinary activities, we should treat each experience and moment as of unique importance. We should seek to maximise each moment. 'Let it not escape from you!' warns the Buddha.

The 'way of mindfulness' draws attention to the vital importance for us of the first stage of perception: the initial 'conscious awareness' of, attention to, or 'taking notice' of people and objects. It is clear that further stages of our perception, for example of things, persons and events in their detail and inter-relationships, are affected by the purity or lack of purity of the initial awareness of the object. Thus, as a first step in the 'way of right mindfulness', we need to cultivate a 'bare attention' or clear and single-minded awareness of what actually happens at successive moments. 'Bare attention' therefore eschews judgement or evaluation in favour of purifying the experience of first impressions. The Buddha is recorded as teaching: 'In what is seen there should only be the seen; in what is heard, only the heard; in what is sensed (as smell, taste or touch) only the sensed; in what is thought, only the thought.' In other words, we are invited to allow things, people and experiences to speak for themselves and we are asked to live in full awareness of the here and now.

I am sure that most of us would freely admit that we live our lives in too much of a hurry to notice so many things. The university college where I teach is in the heart of London surrounded by many of the largest and most fashionable stores as well as many office blocks. The area is full of large crowds in a hurry. Recently I was stopped at the entrance to the college by two passers-by who were admiring the large bronze statue of the Virgin and Child by the eminent sculptor Epstein which graces the front of the building. 'It's funny,' one of them commented, 'I have passed this way every day for many years on the way to work and never noticed that before!' When we go somewhere we are often too concerned about arriving on time or on what is going to happen when we arrive to notice the many sights and sounds on the way – even very large statues!

Yet, as we all experience, we also have to act, choose, decide and judge at almost every moment of the day. In response to this, Buddhism suggests a second aspect of the 'way of mindfulness', called 'clear comprehension', which aims to make all our activities, choices and judgements truly purposeful and in accordance with our ideals. If 'bare attention' focuses on full awareness, 'clear comprehension' seeks a proper understanding of purpose. Is this action really in accordance with my purpose? And am I free from egocentric habits or thought-patterns? 'Clear comprehension' very much depends on allowing the focus of my formal meditation to flow into my daily routine. In the end 'mindfulness' absorbs all activities so that life as a whole becomes 'spiritual practice'.[17]

## The Jesus prayer

Finally, it is worth noting briefly a living Christian tradition which continues to emphasise 'ceaseless prayer' in the tradition of the desert fathers. The 'Jesus prayer' of the Christian East becomes almost habitual and unconscious through continuous repetition. This helps a person to be in God's presence in all places and activities. Given the increasing popularity of this form of prayer in the West, we should be aware that the tradition is far more than a mere mechanical repetition of a phrase ('Lord Jesus Christ, Son of God, have mercy on me') or simply of the name of Jesus and should really be practised only with adequate guidance. In the very popular book *The Way of the Pilgrim* the anonymous author was directed to recite the Jesus prayer up to twelve thousand times a day! 'I roamed about through many different places for a long time with the Prayer of Jesus as my sole companion. It gladdened and comforted me in all my wanderings, my meetings with other people and in all the incidents of the journey.'[18]

The important point is the way that such praying may accompany normal living – the question of quantity mentioned by the 'pilgrim' is in fact unusual. Even the formal recitation during explicit times of prayer has no set length. Perhaps the reference to such an extraordinary number of recitations is in fact a symbolic way of expressing the continuous quality of the overflow of this prayer into every moment of the day. The free recitation is, according to a contemporary writer in the tradition, a way of spiritualising perfectly normal activities such as mending socks, washing up or waiting in a queue.[19]

### Does time have a value?

It may appear that what I have written is tantamount to denying the value of time and solitude in prayer. However we can recall our starting point – how do we respond to the problem of finding time for extended prayer and of linking prayer to everyday life? I do not intend to deny a value to time but rather to put it in proper perspective and, to a degree, to relativise it.

Whether our normal prayer involves regular, formal periods or not, the same basic emphases are important. Firstly, in order to enter the intimacy with God that is offered, it is not necessary to find ways of attracting God's attention or of meriting God's love. It seems to be the case that the deeper our prayer goes, the more we may sense our unworthiness or our need for growth, but equally the more there is a forgetfulness of self which counteracts the tendency to be self-conscious about times for prayer or about length. Such self-consciousness is associated with a belief that prayer is essentially a human activity which we have to improve or 'do well at'. Too often, I feel, we end up believing that we are not good at prayer or that we have somehow failed because we are distracted or dry. Secondly, prayer is frequently seen as a special activity in life that we have to learn and in which we can become more proficient through technique. Prayer, however, is not a matter of proficiency but a living relationship and a *desire* for God. If 'time' and 'times' are basically associated with a belief in technique they are a delusion. In the context of a results-orientated Western society there is something to be learned from the oriental emphasis on letting go of striving and effort. It is said that to achieve 'enlightenment' we must stop trying. A wise Zen *roshi* suggested to a disciple that if he tried hard enlightenment might take five years, but if he tried very, very hard it might take twenty years!

The emphasis on prayer as exclusively a special activity in life may not only lead to an excessive reliance on technique and structure but equally to a sense that time for prayer means time away from life. However, a thorough-going incarnational basis for prayer does not reject the everyday as a distraction. Christian prayer should always involve who and where we are. Many of us have inherited a one-sided 'spirituality of disengagement' which sees life fundamentally as an encumbrance. Here, as I have suggested, the Examen of St Ignatius may help us to appreciate that God is active and present in the most ordinary events of life. It is certainly important for us not to run away from prayer into activism, but it is also important to reinforce our sense that, for exceedingly busy people, the greater part of our prayer will take place outside the time we can infrequently set aside for formal meditation or the like.

It is important, as far as possible, to create oases within a very active life. There is a real danger of fragmentation – of giving less and less attention to more and more things. It seems to be a phenomenon of our age that there is an increasing sense of being pressurised. When I listen to those who are actively involved in the Church it is clear that this pressure has become internalised and is linked to a sense of guilt about taking 'time off' and to a duty to be always available. It often seems to me better to begin by thinking in terms of creating necessary leisure and 'taking time for yourself' in order to achieve a greater personal balance. More 'time for prayer' (if this is an issue) can be tackled later. To address this first before the human question is faced may once again set in motion the treadmill of guilt about religious or ministerial duties.

With some of us, the problem of 'time and times' for prayer may be associated less with guilt than with a genuine call to solitude within an active life. To feel genuinely drawn to extended periods of prayer when circumstances do not permit this may cause real suffering. However, careful discernment is needed here. The genuine call needs to be distinguished from seeking to avoid the demands of everyday life. We have all, no doubt, met people like the seminarian who continually felt drawn to prayer in the chapel at the times when he should have been studying or undertaking ordinary domestic tasks in the service of his companions.

Sometimes we need to expand our understanding of prayer and even to ask questions about the time-cycle within which we think and work. Praying is not incompatible with other activities such as walking and rhythmic domestic tasks such as cleaning or ironing. Other people I know have linked their praying to activities that some people would see simply as hobbies or relaxing pastimes such as playing or listening to music, sketching or carving. Equally, time for prayer should not be reduced to the simple equation 'each day must have a generous quota'. Perhaps in an urban environment people need time-cycles, different from the traditional one of twenty-four hours, which fit in with a more realistic pattern such as term/vacation or with the greater irregularity of holidays or days off now that the traditional weekend or Sunday rest-day is no longer sacrosanct in contemporary Western society.

In the end, whatever we decide about 'time and times' must be rooted in the real situation of each of us and should help us to use to the maximum those opportunities for prayer that actually exist. We should not burden ourselves or other people with a spirituality that condemns us to continual failure or to feelings of being second-rate.

1. See, for example, K. Leech, *The Social God* (London 1981), especially ch. 3.
2. See *Letters of St Ignatius of Loyola*, trans. William Young (Chicago 1959), p. 40 – cited subsequently as *Letters*.
3. Cassian, *Conferences* 10, 10.
4. *The Sayings of the Desert Fathers*, trans. Benedicta Ward (London 1981), p. 121.
5. St Augustine, *Ad Probam*, in Migne, PL 33, col. 1075.
6. St Teresa of Avila, *The Way of Perfection* (London 1961), p. 89.
7. On the development of Jesuit prayer see the useful summary in 'Ignatian Prayer or Jesuit Spirituality' by Joseph Veale in *The Way Supplement* 27 (Spring 1976).
8. *The Spiritual Exercises of St Ignatius*, ed. Louis J. Puhl (Chicago 1951), sections 230–37 – cited subsequently in text as Exx.
9. See G. Aschenbrenner, 'Consciousness Examen' in *Review for Religious*, vol. 31 (1972), pp. 14–21.
10. See Aloysius Pieris, 'Spirituality and Liberation' in *The Month*, April 1983.
11. See M. Giuliani, 'The Ignatian "Exercise" in Daily Life' in *The Way Supplement* 49 (Spring 1984).
12. *Letters*, p. 129.
13. *Letters*, pp. 254–55.
14. *Letters*, p. 211.
15. *Letters*, p. 240.
16. See de Caussade, *The Sacrament of the Present Moment*, trans. K. Muggeridge (London 1981), and Brother Lawrence, *The Practice of the Presence of God*, trans. E. M. Blaiklock (London 1981), especially p. 29.
17. See Nyanaponika Thera, *The Heart of Buddhist Meditation* (London 1972), pp. 24–7.
18. See G. P. Fedotov, *A Treasury of Russian Spirituality* (London 1981), p. 294.
19. See Kallistos Ware, *The Power of the Name* (Fairacres Publications, Oxford, 1980).

# 7
# Prayer and Social Consciousness

I have been concerned to affirm that far from being an activity set apart from everyday life, prayer is intimately connected to it. However, it is possible to accept this in terms of my own private world of home and work without facing the question of the relationship between my Christian life, including prayer, and the wider world, with its varied social issues, of which I am inextricably a part. One of the most striking developments in contemporary spirituality has precisely been the recovery of a sense that the social and ecclesial dimensions of Christian religious experience are not merely an afterthought; that our religious experience is never purely *spiritual* nor purely *individual*. This realisation finds its roots in the Christian tradition about God. In other words, religious experience is essentially communal and involved with the world of ordinary experience precisely because God is social and involved.

The nature of the Christian life is an issue that was at the heart of the debates about the doctrine of the Trinity and Incarnation during the first four centuries of the Christian era. To think of God as a Trinity is fundamentally to assert that within God there is society or community and an equality of relationships. To talk of men and women being created in the image of God implies, therefore, that we are called to share in a divine life that is essentially social. If we go further and talk of an incarnate God, we assert that God took human flesh, entered our human experience and world and that as a result our human nature is raised into the life of God. This involves a rejection of the image of a distant and uninvolved God with which, in practice, many Western Christians work.

In the phrase 'the Word became flesh' exists the basis for a spirituality that is profoundly material and humanist. The earliest diagnostic test or principle of discernment for a truly Christian spirituality is in the First Letter of John (4:2) – 'You can tell the spirits that come from God by this: every spirit which acknowledges that Jesus the Christ has come in the flesh is from God; but any spirit which will not say this of Jesus is not from God . . . ' Thus it would be a profound distortion of Christian spirituality to adopt a low view of the flesh and material things, to see withdrawal or flight as the only appropriate reaction to the world, to think of human nature as fundamentally depraved, and to understand redemption as the salvation of individuals from the world.

A social, involved and incarnate God is the basis for all Christian life. Only if the human Christ is truly united with the divine can there be, through him, real communion with God. Equally, if humanity is taken into God, to be human is to be in communion with others for all are one in God. Then Jesus' statement that 'in so far as you did this to one of the least of these brothers of mine, you did it to me' (Matt. 25:40) becomes a profound theological truth and not merely figurative language. In other words, to assert the essential unity and solidarity of the human race is a theological statement. For the Christian mystic or contemplative, therefore, love of God and love of people are inseparable. The fourteenth-century Flemish mystic Ruusbroec, for example, was quite clear that those who practise the attainment of inner peace as the goal of their prayer and disregard charity or ethics are guilty of spiritual wickedness.[1]

If human solidarity is forgotten, contemplation becomes no more than spiritual self-delusion. A non-social experience, or one that is purely 'spiritual' and removed from our material existence, is a self-centred concern for a false peace. The greatest danger for Christian spirituality is for it to become anti-material, spiritualised, and individualistic (whether removed from a sense of social or Church community). Yet I think it is true that most of us instinctively tend to pray in the 'I' mode, or to focus in the first instance on our own experience, lives and needs. Equally many people find it difficult to experience the reality of God in every element of daily life. Retreat, silence and solitude seem to be the *only* contexts for such experience. The world of ordinary events and feelings merely gets in the way and acts as a distraction. A 'spiritualised' under-standing of religious experience will mean that we are unable to find God in certain elements of our ordinary experience such as anger or suffering, or in the murkier aspects of the wider world. There will be a tendency to retreat into prayer and 'spiritual' experiences as ends in themselves without any obvious implications for our behav-iour and attitudes. It then becomes possible, apparently, to contemplate while remaining socially unaware or, worse, a perpetrator of oppression.

A Sri Lankan theologian very graphically expresses this unhealthy dichotomy between the horizontal and vertical dimensions of life, present in much Christian prayer, by using the image of the statues on the west front of Chartres Cathedral:

> Elongated figures of 'saints' thinned out of the world to reach a God above, and the stout, stocky figures of this-worldly artisans and peasants supporting with the sweat of their brows that other 'leisure class' who have all the time and energy for liturgies and mystical contemplation, point to a conception of spirituality indelibly sculptured in the cathedrals of our collective unconscious.[2]

The link between prayer and social awareness finds its source in two basic things: the interpenetration of religious experience and everyday life, and the essentially communal or social nature of Christian religious experience. Both of these elements are implied by the trinitarian and incar-national ways of understanding God in Christian tradition. Part of our problem with grasping the inherent link between prayer and social awareness, contemplation and engagement, is that we frequently think of God, implicitly at least, in unsatisfactory ways. God is thought of as being in 'a place' or places that are felt to be sacred. Biblically this meant an intimate association with the Temple or with the holy city of Jerusalem as a whole and so on. Gradually the special 'dwelling place of God' as a symbol of God's universal presence in the midst of his people became reduced to certain literal 'sacred places'.

A more sophisticated version of this same problem of distinguishing the sacred from the profane is to think of God as to be found in encounters with the inexplicable. The problem with this approach is that it can soon come to mean no more than the gaps where our powers of explanation falter. As fewer areas remain inexplicable in this way with the advance of human knowledge the 'gaps' where God may be experienced decrease and finally we find no room for God in the whole universe. Another dangerous move from symbolic-imaginative language to the literal can appear in our attempts to express the transcendence of God. Very soon God is 'in the heavens' – distant, remote and infinitely separated from our world. Ultimately, however, Christian tradition understands God as present and acting within all things. God 'is the goal of each thing in its inner dynamism'.[3]

If we understand truly that God is intimately involved in all things, indeed is the inner reality of everything, then it becomes possible to assert that the test of the quality of our prayer is the quality of our life. If we judge prayer merely by feelings (although this is *not* to deny the importance of feelings) we make prayer an end in itself and unconnected with life. The late Jock Dalrymple expressed this in a neat phrase: 'Prayer is the articulated expression of our whole lives.'[4] In other words, prayer is intimately connected with how we live the gospel of Jesus in our lives. Prayer that is unconcerned with the situation of our neighbour is pure self-indulgence. Experience teaches that as people enter more deeply into the mystery of prayer their sensitivities become heightened. Contemplation and conduct may become somewhat blurred and yet prayer remains vitally important. An outstanding Archbishop of Canterbury, William Temple, summed this up in his famous comment that 'The right relation between prayer and conduct is not that conduct is supremely important and prayer helps it, but that prayer is supremely important and conduct is its test'.[5] For it is in prayer that we may be most consciously exposed to God's transforming grace.

*Biblical sources*

I have found that my reflections on the necessity of a link between prayer and social awareness and its nature have been greatly assisted by reference to Scripture. I would like to focus briefly on the beatitudes in the Gospel of Matthew (Matt. 5: 1–12), and the preaching of Jesus about the nature of the Kingdom of God. In a sense each beatitude contains within itself all the others, but the sixth ('Blessed are the pure of heart, for they shall see God') appears to speak most directly to our concern with prayer – for what is contemplation if not 'seeing God'? For this reason we may take this phrase as somehow summing up the rest. Those who see God truly are those who are 'pure of heart'. Our problem with the word 'pure' is that we think of moral purity in the narrow sense. Psalm 24 (verse 4) suggests that a 'pure heart' is associated with 'clean hands'; the two elements are inseparable facets of the same purity. Equally this kind of purity involves not paying 'homage to worthless things'; that is, the cutting off of all forms of idolatry. Finally the same psalm verse talks of not swearing 'so as to deceive our neighbour'. We are to uproot all deceit from our hearts.

To return to the beatitudes in Matthew, it is possible therefore to see 'pure hands' as intimately linked with a pure heart; exterior attitudes and actions must be consonant with our inner dispositions. Inner integrity is certainly central to holiness but it cannot be its sum total. Thus Christian contemplation, as a following of Jesus and a living experience of God in Jesus, transcends the kind of religious experience that merely satisfies 'religious' sentiment without producing a radical reorientation of life.[6]

Old Testament prophecy provides a good model for seeing the closest possible link between ethics and a true spirituality. 'He judged the cause of the poor and needy, then it was well with him. Was not this to know me? says the Lord' (Jer. 22:16). The link between false worship and a lack of concern for the poor and weak is underlined by the prophecies of Amos (e.g. 5:22–4) and Isaiah (e.g. 1:12–17) and of course in those verses from Micah (6:6–8)

that have become favourites with people seeking a biblical
basis for a more 'social' spirituality:

> 'With what gift shall I come into Yahweh's presence
> and bow down before God on high? Shall I come with
> holocausts, with calves one year old? Will he be pleased
> with rams by the thousand, with libations of oil in
> torrents? Must I give my first-born for what I have done
> wrong, the fruit of my body for my own sin?' What is
> good has been explained to you . . . ; this is what Yahweh
> asks of you: only this, to act justly, to love tenderly, and
> to walk humbly with your God.

This prophetic tradition concerning true worship may be
linked with Jesus' preaching of the Kingdom. The
Kingdom of God involves a movement away from false
security and being at ease. In essence it is about a change
of vision and the power of God to change people and
situations. In the gospels, the Kingdom experience is
expressed essentially as a real change in the human
condition: the lifeless stir, the blind see, paralysis is cured.
And beyond the human, physical facts is the deeper invitation to conversion of which the physical events act as
signs and stimuli. The Kingdom in Jesus' teaching and
action is not an interior spiritual matter only. It is set to
transform the face of the earth and of human history. The
acid test of the truly converted heart is expressed in such
terms as 'Seek justice, correct oppression, defend the
fatherless, plead for the widow' (Isa. 1:17) or as the recognition of Jesus in the hungry, naked and prisoners (Matt.
25). Therefore the search for the face of God is practical –
it is nonsense to praise and worship a God who we believe
is present everywhere and to ignore him in the specific –
in the 'somewhere' or the 'someone'.

## Contemplation as engagement

A number of contemporary writers both on contemplation
and on Christian social engagement remind us that neither
activity can survive without the other. In the past there
was a tendency to present withdrawal, solitude, the desert
and contemplation as one polarity and action, mission,

engagement as another. We desperately need to recover the fullness of the Christian tradition whereby both withdrawal *and* engagement will be held together in tension. Without engagement or social consciousness, contemplation runs the danger of becoming disembodied interiority. Without contemplation, engagement may mean merely restless activity or another ideology.

Such writers as the Cistercian monk, Thomas Merton or the American Jesuit peace activist, Daniel Berrigan remind us that the pursuit of a prayerful life and of simple love and discipleship inevitably opposes us to the mainstream of materialist culture. The trouble with much contemporary spirituality is that its emphasis on direct experience, good feelings, joy, praise and peace (while not of course bad in themselves) is not always accompanied by contemplative struggle, conflict with a fallen world, solidarity with the whole of humanity and preaching the Kingdom of God in its full radicality.

Daniel Berrigan speaks of contemplation as a truly subversive activity and as a '*political act*' that, because engaged with the ambiguities of human existence, is fundamentally risky.[7] This kind of contemplation is not only compatible with resistance to all that dehumanises, but necessarily involves it. The mystical and the prophetic dimensions of Christian life and witness, like withdrawal and engagement, are not to be seen as mutually exclusive but as interpenetrating – even if particular people emphasise one element more than the other in their choice of lifestyle. Two Christian victims of the Nazi terror in Germany during the 1940s witness particularly forcefully to this truth. Alfred Delp, the famous Jesuit preacher and spiritual director, was a genuine contemplative who reflected from his prison cell, shortly before being executed, that 'great issues facing mankind have to be decided in the wilderness, in uninterrupted isolation and unbroken silence. They hold a meaning and a blessing, these great, silent, empty spaces that bring man face to face with reality.'[8] Like Delp, Dietrich Bonhoeffer, the Lutheran pastor and theologian also executed by the Nazis in the aftermath of the bomb plot against Hitler in 1944, wove together a consistent resistance to oppression and dehumanisation with a deeply prayerful and, one might say, contemplative attitude. There is something profoundly symbolic in the fact that he prepared for his impending death during a period of enforced solitude and wilderness in a cell at the Abbey of Ettal.

It is hardly surprising that Thomas Merton, as a monk, believed in the importance of solitude and silence – but not as ends in themselves, for 'in solitude, in the depths of man's own aloneness lie the resources for resistance to injustice'.[9] Not, however, that the early Merton would have spoken in this way. His initial, absolute, search for world-renunciation led him to feel positively uncomfortable with his surroundings on his infrequent trips into the nearby town – not to mention superior to the unfortunate people he saw who had not yet found his inner peace. Merton had to experience a radical conversion before he could write of the intimate connection between contemplation and engagement, the desert and struggle. He expresses this conversion quite graphically. 'In Louisville . . . in the centre of the shopping district, I was suddenly over-whelmed with the realisation that I loved all these people, that they were mine, and I theirs. That we could not be alien to one another even though we were total strangers. It was like waking from a dream of separateness, of furious self-isolation in a special world – the world of renunciation and supposed holiness.'[10]

## The prayer of the desert

All of the people I have mentioned came to realise that any resistance to inhumanity that was not wrought out of a deep inner struggle must remain superficial. But equally they realised the need for contemplation to have some integrity. The aloneness with God which Jesus experienced when he was led into the wilderness was not for its own sake. He was in the desert to be tempted. In much of the Christian tradition, the desert has been seen as a symbol of withdrawal. We need to recover another perspective – that the desert is also a place of struggle and purification. Whether it is St Ignatius Loyola in his *Spiritual Exercises* or Thomas Merton, Christian tradition has always seen the presence of conflict and struggle as in some sense a sign of the validity of prayer experience and of the reality of spiritual growth. Inner conflict marks a vital difference between true solitude and silence on the one hand, and the false comfort of disengagement on the other.

Spiritual experience or prayer are not defences against the challenge of being human in an ambiguous world. A bogus spirituality will be self-centred and evade risk and tension. The solitude of the desert and the prayer of the desert, therefore, will not be experiences of security. Rather they strip us of illusion and invite us to leave the many false selves with which we face the world and indeed ourselves. In solitude we cannot, for long, run away from reality – whether the truth about ourselves or about our world. The symbol of the desert, at its most powerful, is about seeing truly. The mirage of material security, power and honour are seen to be temptations.

True contemplation, therefore, results in a transformation of vision. When we contemplate, far from being escapists, we gradually become people who see more clearly. Indeed, as some have suggested, too clearly for comfort. Experience teaches that the deeper we go in prayer and the more truly contemplative that prayer becomes, the greater the pain of reality. Certainly, if we are to believe the great mystics, there is a deepening awareness of personal unworthiness (accompanied by an equal increase in the sense of God's mercy and unmerited love). But equally, I have found, people talk about an increase of sensitivity about *all* reality. This sensitivity is not limited to the joyful and pleasurable – a recognition of the beauty of God in nature, in people, in events. It also frequently includes a great deal of pain as the darker side of reality impinges more strongly on the sensitised consciousness.

*Contemplation and self-forgetfulness*

If true Christian contemplation leads us to desire not inner peace for its own sake (crying 'peace, peace' where there is no peace) but the coming of the fullness of the Kingdom, the sensitivity which it brings also involves an increase of love. When we come to see truly, we do so in and through love. And it is this love which provides both the inner strength to maintain resistance against the forces of evil in the face of overwhelming odds, and also that freedom from self-seeking which will eschew fanatical ideology. The latter is an inherent danger in any social commitment that lacks contemplative vision. The division between contemplation and social commitment is for this reason unfortunate and highly dangerous. Certainly a rejection of spiritualities that preach a blind and selfish interiority is understandable and valid. But contemplation of the kind I have described is at the very root of a truly Christian approach to social justice. Without a contemplative awareness we cease to see people (whether the oppressed or the oppressors) and instead react in an impersonal way.

Segundo Galilea, a priest from Chile who has written extensively about spirituality from a liberation theology perspective, talks about a movement from an initially 'ethical' response to social situations towards a truly 'spiritual experience' – the discovery in the poor of God's compassion and of the humanity of Christ.[11] Galilea emphasises the contemplative dimension of the search for social justice. First of all, he suggests, there is a fundamental rediscovery of the gospel experience of Jesus, his attitudes and his call to follow him. This is vital, for our attitude to the poor and also to the oppressors cannot be complete unless we learn from Jesus. We cannot have true compassion without entering into Jesus' own compassion. Contemplation also helps to bring about that change of heart without which there can be no lasting justice or solidarity. Social engagement must be accompanied by a process of inner freedom from sin and self-seeking. Thus liberation theology emphasises not a purely political, economic or social analysis but what is often called 'integral liberation': that is, a way of seeing and acting which unites the search for social change and inner conversion of heart.

The condition of true contemplation, as of true Christian engagement, must be to leave behind a selfish centring on my own experience in isolation. I have already suggested that contemplation cannot be an end in itself, and neither should our desire for a deeper union with God. This comment, of course, is nothing new. St Augustine, for example, cited charity as the fundamental purpose of the contemplative life. A contemporary theologian, Moltmann, provides a helpful way of understanding this when he suggests that there is a kind of continuous circular movement between our social concern or action and our growth in deeper union with God. This movement is described in terms of five stages or moments. Our initial response to any need that we see is to act to change things. Such action inevitably leads us to a realisation that any truly *Christian* response has to be supported by meditation. Meditation on the history of Jesus in the gospels leads eventually to the awareness of the Spirit of God within us leading slowly to our full humanity, to conversion, to becoming people more and more in God's image. In other words, contemplation leads ultimately to a movement away from self and also from false images of God to the true God and to God alone. To encounter the living God and to be purified of our selfishness is what we mean by union, but this 'union' is not an end in itself. We are not called to remain in some kind of pure spiritual experience removed from responsibility and now beyond concern with ordinary life. Thus mysticism or contemplation leads back to discipleship. For Christian contemplation, as opposed to some other oriental forms, finds its source in the crucified Jesus and leads us therefore to an identification with the Jesus who moves out of himself in compassion and self-giving love. 'As long as we do not think that dying with Christ spiritually is a substitute for dying with him in reality, mysticism does not mean estrangement from action; it is a preparation for public, political discipleship.'[12]

*Conclusion*

What I have described so far I have done in objective terms. I have tried to suggest that prayer and social consciousness or engagement are not two quite separate and indeed competing experiences. Withdrawal and engagement are not mutually exclusive but rather are complementary values. There is certainly a tension which cannot be resolved simply; indeed must be maintained, because it is the very dialectic between contemplation and action which prevents either from becoming self-centred and which insures that in both experiences there is a call to continual conversion. I would like to end by describing two personal experiences which illustrate what I mean.

Some years ago I spent about eight months living and studying in India. This was the first time in my life that I had spent such a long period so far away from my home and friends. Apart from missing familiar companions during the first couple of months I was also very aware of the physical distance that separated me from a number of other people whom I had been trying to help in a variety of ways. The inability to be physically present to these people left me with a feeling of powerlessness. What I came to realise was that in so many ways I *needed* to be present to these people and to be the person who helped them. It was force of circumstances that made me let go of this need. All I found that I could do was to offer people, simply and trustfully, to God in prayer; to ask God to be for them what I could not be at the time. Obviously this was merely a first step, for I gradually came to realise that this open offering to God should always be at the centre of our involvement with and caring for others. But it is so easy to forget in practice when we are present to people in a direct way. I also came to experience in prayer that my physical non-presence became less and less important as I experienced a reality of presence to people, places and situations, in God, that was far more intense while more free than had been the case in my more direct attempts to be of assistance. In this way, I believe, I learned a great deal about the way that prayer, far from leading us away from engagement, makes a qualitative difference to the way we are present to people and situations. It transforms our perceptions and challenges the unacknowledged personal needs that so often stand in the way of being truly present.

More recently I was involved in group retreat with fellow Jesuits. In one of our daily periods of sharing prayer experiences we discussed the fact that, instinctively, our personal prayer was in the 'I' mode and that it tended to begin and end with our own inner experience. Certainly we tried to move outwards but this was always more difficult. We wondered whether praying in the first person singular all the time tended to predetermine the direction in which our prayer developed. As a result we agreed to try to pray in the first person plural, the 'we' mode. If we were using Scripture, for example a psalm, as the starting point for prayer we would 'translate' the singular language into the plural. Initially we found this very difficult because so unfamiliar, and yet we persisted over several days. In the end the effect was quite striking. Not only did we eventually slip into the plural form fairly easily but the focus of our prayer and its direction changed noticeably. The wider world was no longer 'out there', distinct from the inner world of the 'I'. Using the 'we' form forced us to begin from within the wider world. Our inner experience, while in no sense excluded, began to feel quite different as a result.

These two experiences illustrate in a quite simple way (or, at least, they do to me) that contemplation and engagement can be brought together into a fruitful dialogue which inevitably changes the structure of both. True Christian engagement is the product of a contemplative vision. Contemplation provides that heightened sensitivity which makes us increasingly aware of the way things really are both within ourselves and in the situations of need which we encounter. In reverse, contemplation does not take place in a vacuum but has a necessary context in the concrete world of the everyday.

1. See for example John Ruusbroec, *The Spiritual Espousals*, book 2, 'The Interior Life', in the Ruusbroec volume in the Classics of Western Spirituality (New York 1985), pp. 136–43 *passim*.
2. Aloysius Pieris, 'Spirituality and Liberation' in *The Month*, April 1983, p. 120.
3. See John Wright, *A Theology of Christian Prayer* (New York 1979), p. 45.
4. John Dalrymple, *Simple Prayer* (London 1984), p. 65.
5. Quoted in Dalrymple, op.cit., p. 67.
6. For a stimulating study of the beatitudes as a model for pastoral theology see: Segundo Galilea, *The Beatitudes: to Evangelise as Jesus Did* (New York 1984).
7. Daniel Berrigan, *America is Hard to Find* (London 1973), pp. 77–8.
8. The extract from Delp's prison meditations is quoted in Leech, *The Social God* (London 1981), p. 41.

9. James Douglass, *Resistance and Contemplation* (New York 1972), p. 139.
10. Thomas Merton, *Conjectures of a Guilty Bystander* (London 1977), p. 153.
11. Segundo Galilea, 'The Spirituality of Liberation' in *The Way*, July 1985, pp. 186–94.
12. Jürgen Moltmann, *Experiences of God* (London 1980), p. 73.

# 8
## Imagination and Prayer

---

I would like to end these reflections on discipleship and prayer with one that is more explicitly practical. In recent years many people, seeking to deepen or expand their experience of prayer, have found great help in what is called gospel contemplation. I have pleaded previously for a recovery of the tradition that prayer need not involve extended periods of solitude and meditation. So it may seem a paradox to conclude by discussing a way of praying that clearly demands these things. However, I do not reject the importance of solitude and time, I merely believe that these should be relativised. The value of gospel contemplation is that, in a particularly fruitful way, it can bring together some of the elements on which I have focused in previous chapters. First of all, as contemplation precisely on Scripture and particularly the gospels, it can take us into the very heart of the call to discipleship. It has also proved a very powerful means, as I have already hinted in 'Images of God', of bringing us into contact with our inner desires, fears and barriers to growth. Finally it has provided, for many people, a reinforcement of a more socially conscious prayer by challenging them to see the world in a new way.

Stated very simply, gospel contemplation consists in taking a scene from the gospels, and 'putting myself in the midst of the action', or making it present through the use of the imagination. Perhaps the easiest way to explain how gospel or imaginative contemplation proceeds is to begin by describing some of the experiences of retreatants I have known. The experiences are true but for the sake of confidentiality I have changed some of the personal details. There was, firstly, a school teacher who had never tried this way

of praying before. She was asked to use the incident of
Peter walking on the water (Matt. 14:22–33). When she
came to describe her experience of prayer, she said that to
start with she had no difficulty in imagining herself in a
boat, as she had in fact been sailing as a youngster. She
knew what it was like to experience the frustration and
fear of fighting against a strong wind and current. This
helped her to 'get inside' the scene. She recognised that
Jesus was there and found herself, like Peter, with a strong
desire to join him, to be alongside him. However, she also
felt unable to get out of the boat. Try as she might, she
could not imagine herself doing this 'and so the prayer
went wrong at that point'. Why did she feel this? 'Because,
up to then, I could identify with the actual story in the
gospel but when I could not get out of the boat it all broke
down'. And so what did she do? 'I said to Jesus, "I can't
get out of this boat".' Then she felt that Jesus was asking
her whether she thought that he would make her do something beyond her capacity. 'Yes you would . . . you often
have.' This experience led the person to spend the
remainder of the prayer sitting and talking to Christ about
the fact that she did not really trust him because she did
not know him well enough.

This example, it seems to me, underlines with great
clarity some of the more important elements of the imaginative kind of prayer. Most importantly, the woman was
fully involved and not just a spectator observing a picture,
as one might contemplate a painting in a gallery. Quite
instinctively she found herself identifying with one of the
characters in the gospel scene. And yet she did not *become*
Peter, she remained herself. In this sense she did not put
herself back in time. Rather, the story became present, and
became *her* story. In this case she found it easy to enter
the scene by some initially detailed imagination of being
in a boat. However, as the story progressed, the degree of
pictorial imagination grew less and less. Those with a
strong ability to picture details find the notion of seeing
the people, or feeling the wind on the face, or smelling the
fish in the bottom of the boat very easy indeed. However,
this is not a necessary part of imaginative prayer. Pictorial
imagination is only one way of imagining. Not all are

capable of it, and not all find it necessary. The woman in question, as the story progressed, found that this aspect was less apparent. She 'sensed' that Jesus was asking her something, rather than heard specific words coming from a figure whom she could visualise and describe. This fact is important because some people object to trying imaginative contemplation precisely because they feel unable to imagine pictorially, or because it is unreal. Likewise, for those who do find it possible and helpful, there is the danger of becoming too involved in the trivia which, if used at all, are only means to an end. That end, of course, is some kind of personal encounter with the Lord which touches the deepest parts of my reality. And that encounter was really present for this woman, in that the imaginative representation of a particular scene provoked a realisation of something very vital to her relationship with Christ: that she did not trust. Did the prayer go wrong because it ceased to follow the gospel story in literal detail? On the contrary, the gospel was a medium for the revelation of something very important and true about herself. And yet the gospel story was not left behind entirely. It was this specific scene of walking on the water which formed the backdrop to everything else that was valid about the prayer. And the prayer certainly remained within the general parameters of the gospel passage.

Another characteristic of this form of prayer is that it can free a person to allow deep-rooted feelings to emerge which are blocking any further growth. Imaginative contemplation, when it progresses naturally, takes on a life of its own – and the life is that of the person praying. It therefore serves to bring the gospel into direct contact with the reality of this person's life, and frequently in a challenging way. Such prayer may also help a person come to terms with, and admit to, inner feelings which previously he or she felt were inappropriate before God. 'I should not feel angry.' A more distanced approach to Scripture, where one asks, 'What did Jesus say? What did he mean? How does this apply to Christian action?' rarely does this. For when one is bringing only reason to the gospels there is a tendency to apply *a priori* limits to what is valid.

Another retreatant, in praying the calming of the storm

in Mark (4:36–41), was brought face to face both with what she felt about Christ and how she herself behaved in life. Jesus, lying at the bottom of the boat, was in the way as she rushed around trimming the sails in the midst of the squall. At first she was politely apologetic at bumping into him, but eventually she shouted at him, 'What do you think you are doing there? Lolling around when we have to do all the work? Why don't you do something useful?' To which the only reply was, 'Who is in charge here anyway?' This brought the person to a halt and led her to reflect that this imaginative experience, unlike simply thinking about the gospel, underlined both her feelings that God was generally uninvolved in her concerns, and that, in fact, she rarely let God act because she did not let go or relax either in life or in prayer. A similar realisation came to the person who prayed the call of the first disciples in John (1:35–9). When Jesus asked him 'What do you seek?', his instinctive response was 'To be with you'. Jesus then invited the man in question to follow, and set off at a rapid pace which prevented him from keeping up. When he cried 'Why do you have to go so fast?' Jesus merely smiled and kept going, up hill and down dale and eventually into a town in whose winding streets the man finally lost sight of Jesus. Final panic set in, but with it came the realisation that the problem was that he felt that Christ was always too fast for him, and that consequently his life was always a struggle to keep up with impossible demands.

The realisation of 'impossible demands' raises the question as to whether all images which emerge from such gospel contemplation are true. If we take an example which I have already mentioned of someone who felt in prayer that Jesus said to him 'I'm not going to start loving you until you learn how to love me', it is clear that this is not a truly Christian image of God. As I have suggested, we all come to prayer with images – of God, of self and of our world – but none of them is perfect and some are radically unhelpful. Does this mean that the feeling just described (that God demands that we merit his love) is *totally* untrue? It is true, surely, in that it is what the person actually feels. Distorted images cannot just be repressed; they can only be refined if exposed, admitted to, and offered to God. But such an image is not from God for, if we follow the sound advice of St Ignatius of Loyola's 'Rules for discernment', we can see that what produces joy, harmony and growth is the gift of the good spirit, and that which produces sadness, despair or fragmentation is (to use Ignatius's language) a temptation of the evil spirit.[1]

While the most common approach to imagination in prayer is that of gospel contemplation, it sometimes happens that imagination comes into play in other forms of scripture prayer. Thus I may pray through a slow meditative reading of a passage – associated with what was traditionally called *lectio divina* in monastic spirituality.[2] When a phrase or word strikes me I cease reading and allow myself to savour it for a time until it fills my consciousness and I am fully centred on it. Then, when I feel drawn to respond, I may converse with God in a personal way for as long as seems suitable. I may feel drawn in the end to remain still and silent before returning to the slow reading. The original savouring of the word or phrase does not imply reasoning about its meaning, but rather a process of letting it sink in – perhaps by repetition. However, sometimes the imagery of the Scripture may find an echo in my own imagination. Once again an example may serve to make this point clearer. Someone was using Luke, chapter 13, for prayer and was struck very much by the phrase 'I do not know where you come from' (verse 27). Quite spontaneously he found himself, in imagination, ejected into the rain from a party because the host had said 'I don't believe we have met, and this party is only for friends of mine'. The feeling of isolation, and how it can destroy a person, was further reinforced by imagining a discussion with others who had been refused entry, where they spent the time disparaging the host to cover up their own feelings. When the man imagined himself trying to get home by sharing a taxi with another, he found himself turned away yet again with the words 'I don't believe we are going in the same direction'. This imaginative experience, quite unanticipated, helped the man to reach a deep understanding of some kind of self-made hell. He felt drawn to remain with this, in order to let it penetrate more deeply, and then to converse with Christ about the realisation that

he had been offered so many opportunities to recognise
Jesus and to be recognised by him. 'I always come to you
in prayer as a gate-crasher at a party, but in fact you
always do let me in.' Thus this imaginative experience,
provoked by the phrase in Luke's gospel, led the man to
deep feelings of repentance, and to a realisation of God's
mercy and faithfulness which were in no sense merited.

Apart from indicating a further way in which imagination may, quite spontaneously, play a role in prayer, the
last example also underlines a general point: that imagination is not an end in itself. Its value is that it can dispose
me for an encounter with the living Christ who speaks
directly to my present condition. Once that meeting
between Christ and my inner desires or fears or ambiguities
has begun, the process of imagining ceases to be important
and should not be sustained artificially. In practice a
person will be drawn into dialogue, or into silent 'being
with' the God whose presence is now consciously felt. The
imaginative phase, strictly so-called, may last for most of
the period of prayer or be a relatively brief experience as
a preface to extended silence. The point is that if I believe
that it is God and not I who controls my prayer, I shall
feel quite free to allow myself to be led wherever the Spirit
wishes.

It now seems possible to attempt a summary of the
method of imaginative contemplation in a few words.[3] In
my experience it is important for the freedom of this prayer
not to have to refer back continually to the gospel text for
more information. In other words, I would assume that a
person has become familiar with the passage to be used
before entering into prayer. The text can then be left aside.
In a retreat one normally advises someone to prepare the
passage some time before (often the previous evening) by
reading it through several times and allowing it to sink in.
For some people it is important at this stage to sort out
more theoretical questions such as the meaning of the text
in order to prevent this intruding into the prayer itself.
Something similar may well suit people who want to use
this kind of prayer in daily life. Writers such as John Veltri
and others suggest another more systematic approach as a
prelude to the prayer time.[4] This consists in reading the

passage slowly and meditatively and then stopping to let
the events sink in and repeating this process until it totally
saturates the imagination. Once this has happened the
Bible may be put aside and the scene be permitted to
'happen'. There should be no attempt to force it, but rather
there should be an attentiveness to its developments. As
you sink into the scene you may well experience a loss of
a sense of self as you become more absorbed. The essential
thing is to take part in the process of development. It is
also important to avoid moralising, or forcing applications
of the passage to your life. Nor should you observe how
you are affected by the passage, by asking yourself 'What
is happening to me here?' Rather, you should allow yourself
to be lost in the story – that is to say, in the people, in the
words and in the actions. Your own reactions or 'what
happens to you' will be noticeable later as you reflect back
on the prayer, or perhaps will appear more subtly in the
effect such prayer has on your ordinary life.

While the prayer of imagination undoubtedly has
connections with some of the insights of modern psychology
(especially Jung's 'active imagination'), it is worth
stressing that it is not a contemporary invention but has a
long history in Christian tradition. The medium through
which gospel contemplation has come through to our own
times is the *Spiritual Exercises* of Ignatius Loyola.[5] Until
serious research into Ignatian texts and other sources
became more widespread and systematic in modern times,
imagination tended to be associated with a rather rigid
and dry form of mental prayer or 'meditation' which
involved, above all, the reason and will and which, it was
believed, was the only authentic Ignatian prayer. It is
now appreciated much more widely that Ignatius did not
promote any *one* method of prayer. The Exercises contain
many different ones. Further, we now appreciate more
clearly that the form of imaginative prayer which Ignatius
recommends in the Exercises is really closer to contemplative prayer than to the method of meditation associated
with reason, thinking or will-power which was for many
years presented as somehow uniquely Ignatian prayer.
This view is reinforced if we bear in mind its origins in the
medieval monastic *lectio divina* or meditative reflection on

scripture leading to contemplation. In his teaching on ways of prayer Ignatius is derivative and broadly based rather than narrow. His originality lay in adapting and simplifying the riches of Christian prayer in order to make them accessible beyond the confines of the cloister, and in weaving the various methods into a wider framework, the Exercises, which was conceived as a context to enable a person to reach such an inner freedom that he or she could respond wholeheartedly to the call of Christ in everyday life.

One word of warning. The 'rediscovery' of imaginative contemplation and the realisation that meditation of a more reasoning and active kind is not the only authentic Ignatian prayer has led, in some quarters, to an excess of enthusiasm. We must not fall into the trap of simply replacing meditation with imaginative prayer as somehow uniquely Ignatian! Nor would I want to suggest that to pray the Scriptures imaginatively is vital in order to make St Ignatius' Spiritual Exercises or to enter sympathetically into the Ignatian approach to spirituality.

Ignatius learned the practice of imaginative contemplation from his reading of the *Life of Christ* by Ludolph of Saxony (a fourteenth-century Carthusian), while recovering from the wound he had received at the seige of Pamplona.[6] Ludolph gives the essentials of the method in his prologue where he recommends the reader to look at the events of Christ's life as if they were actually taking place in the present. He himself inherited the tradition from the *Meditations on the life of Christ* which were extremely popular in the fourteenth century and which, while not by Bonaventure as originally supposed, reflected the Franciscan tradition of devotion to the human person of Christ. It is not clear when this form of imaginative prayer actually began but aspects of it are present in the writings of Anselm and Aelred of Rievaulx. Thus the tradition seems to have been passed from the Cistercians to the Franciscans and Carthusians. It is also mentioned favourably by Walter Hilton and Teresa of Avila who reacted strongly against those spiritual directors who suggested that to meditate on the human Christ was a hindrance to deeper prayer.

Some of the reasons why people, including myself in the

past, have found the idea of imaginative prayer difficult were really misunderstandings of the whole process. As I have already suggested, gospel contemplation does not depend on our ability to imagine pictorially. Further, such prayer does not mean being in control of the process, being logical or somehow reproducing the gospel text exactly as it is and in an artificial way. If we are truly involved, the process will inevitably 'take on a life of its own'. Is there a danger of sentimentality? Indeed there is, but all forms of prayer have their dangers, and the objection to this kind of prayer often relates to our problems about using images at all or about the value of feelings. Certainly our prayer should be free from any straining after emotional reactions that do not arise of themselves. However, many of us were originally taught to distrust *any* feelings in prayer, and this needs to be corrected. We come to prayer as whole persons, with body, mind and feelings. To exclude, arbitrarily, one or the other part is to risk the danger of an incomplete response.

Surely, however, imageless prayer is better prayer? Certainly there are not a few modern writings that give this impression. It is worth reflecting once again that imagination played a significant role in the medieval monastic and contemplative tradition. To suggest that praying the gospels gets in the way of reaching out to a God who is beyond all images is to undervalue the 'sacramental' quality of Scripture and the Christian belief that the gospels are a privileged context for encountering the living, risen Jesus. To focus on the person of Christ is hardly a side-track from seeking the God who transcends all our concepts and imaginings. For 'It is the Father's will that whoever sees the Son and believes in him shall have eternal life' (John 6:40). The way to the Father is in Christ: 'No one can come to the Father except through me . . . To have seen me is to have seen the Father' (John 14:6, 9). In talking, therefore, of 'imageless prayer' one has to distinguish carefully between those of us who are *drawn* into silence and stillness, and those who merely feel bound to adopt still, imageless prayer as a matter of principle. Undoubtedly there is a process of simplification by which people need images and ideas less and less as a stimulus for prayer, but this needs some guidance. However, one also needs to remember that progress in prayer is not a matter of straight lines. The need for imagination or some similar starting point recurs at different times even for profound mystics.

Is imagination 'unreal' however? As far as imagining the gospels is concerned, it is a process of making present to myself what is at the deepest level a mystery. For God, all is eternally 'now', and therefore it follows that I can speak to God as present not merely in the imagination but in reality. Scripture, we should remember, has a symbolic quality. That is, the events, parables or miracles recorded are, even if factual in particular instances, more than *mere* facts. There is an open-ended quality to the gospels which points beyond the level of event to universal significance. By universal I do not mean, of course, that there is *one* meaning, but rather that there is a significance which confronts 'all manner and condition of persons'. The significance is a person, Jesus Christ, who is re-presented through the imaginative process. We are not, therefore, talking about going back in time in prayer, but rather entering into the eternal present. There is a parallel with the 'making present' associated with the Eucharist. The risen Lord, though beyond time, enters our experience at this specific moment, and brings the Easter mystery to life for us, and in us, in the Eucharist. Thus too, in imaginative prayer, the Lord can make the mysteries of his life, death and resurrection present to us in their significance now. Is there a contradiction between confronting Christ now, the Jesus of faith, and going back to the Jesus of history? The fact is that we cannot truly distinguish the one from the other. 'The eternal Christ is not just the product or after-math of his thirty years at Nazareth, he *is* this history now'.[7]

Nor is imagination unreal in psychological terms. Jung's method of 'active imagination', in which he encouraged patients to write down, reflect upon or paint their dreams, was based on the belief that one could bring about a healthy interaction between the conscious individual and his unconscious depths.[8] This leads to an enlargement of consciousness by admitting into it feelings or ideas from the unconscious. It is sometimes a question of activating things, for example knowledge and trust, which we already possess deep down. And as a believer I can see that to reach down into my centre is not merely to confront inner feelings and reactions, but to meet God where God is most certainly to be found. The process of revealing my inner feelings and reactions is vital if my prayer is to deepen and grow. I may not be aware of them or, rather, I may not have been prepared to acknowledge them, and for this reason I am only able to meet God with a part of myself. A great deal more is safely locked away. Imaginative prayer, especially when it involves a confrontation with the gospels, frequently serves to brings these feelings to the surface in a creative way.

I have found that some people wonder how gospel contemplation, or prayer with Scripture in general, relates to the insights of contemporary approaches to the text of the Bible. Because this is a complex question I can only hope to make some very general remarks here.[9] First, an important guiding principle is that it is *not* a question of trying to reach the purely historical circumstances of a passage because that would raise problems of its own about relating such a circumscribed experience to our present situation. The gospel texts are the result of a particular writer's experience of the risen Christ, related to the various traditions which the writer has inherited about the Jesus of history. Thus the value of gospel prayer is not the historicity of particular events in the gospels. Rather the experience of the risen Jesus speaks through the gospel tradition to us when we pray or read Scripture. Our access to Jesus through scripture prayer or reading is always mediated through the perspective of the gospel writer, and this perspective involves many layers of meaning. To reach the historical involves passing through other layers: the gospel-writer's own insights, and behind these the oral tradition of the early Christian communities. The value of a gospel text to us does not lie merely at the level of the original historical events but rather each level has its own validity and usefulness. Sometimes, even with the aid of the most sophisticated knowledge of a gospel text we cannot peal back the different layers to reach an original historical event or the undoubted words of Jesus. Maybe we think that scripture scholarship is the ally of imaginative gospel prayer precisely because it seeks out the historical, geographical, cultural, religious, *factual* elements, which then assist the vividness and realism of our experience in praying the passage. I think that this tends to link imagination too narrowly to the historical. We should not forget that imagination is a *creative* not a 'scientific' faculty. The value of modern scripture scholarship to imaginative prayer is that it reveals precisely that the early Christian community mediated the traditions about Jesus in a creative and reflective way. This freedom to be creative is surely a liberating example for contemplative gospel prayer.

I hope it will now be reasonably clear what are some of the particular values of imaginative prayer without claiming too much for it. Within the actual prayer experience there is the fact that Scripture can become alive, often for the first time. This 'coming alive' often involves the imagination in moving beyond the literal text, while remaining within the general parameters of the gospel passage. Thus it brings the person praying to some very deep personal insights both about self and the relationship with God or the world. Because the process of imagining is not the same as analysing the texts, the result is often strikingly simple. That is to say that, on reflection, we may find that the very varied imaginative experience really centres around one single point. Most important of all, perhaps, is the fact that such prayer *involves* us and draws in – indeed involvement is of its very essence. And because I am involved personally, the process of putting myself in the scene is equivalent to 'putting myself on the line' – that is, exposing myself to the transforming presence of Christ.

While some people find this form of prayer helpful as a regular 'method', personally speaking I have only used it as an occasional pattern in recent years, but when used or when it arises spontaneously it has been a challenging prayer, in that it brings me face to face not only with what God wishes to communicate at a particular time, but also with the need to respond and with things within myself that hold me back. Such a response is not merely a matter of pious sentiments for, because such prayer deals directly with life and experience, it cannot be separated from the way I am involved in the world. Unless I am unaware of a social dimension to my existence or rigidly exclude the social dimension of my life from such prayer, contemplation will help to shape, or at least to illuminate the world within which I must function.[10] Jesus' miracles and parables, for example, invite us to change our world-view, and gospel contemplation can increase our awareness of the world as it really is, with its injustices as well as its beauty, and of what God is saying to us in the present about our world.

Gospel contemplation, because it brings us face to face with our response to God and with what is preventing a whole-hearted 'yes', inevitably relates closely to how we are responding or failing to respond to God's plan and to the action of God's love in our lives. Thus such prayer, while contemplative, is also necessarily practical. When I have used gospel contemplation it has often proved of great value in deepening my engagement both with what is going on in myself and also how I am relating to the world around me. Such prayer does not focus on ideas in the abstract or on the theoretical aspects of following Jesus but rather on my honest reactions and feelings in the light of the gospel. Because of this, it has taught me to trust experience, to trust *this* moment and every moment as a privileged encounter with God. Sometimes the experience may be joyful, sometimes it may be quite a struggle with conflicting feelings, doubts or fears. But whatever the experience, I have found that it affirms that 'it is good to be here'. I can learn powerfully that God accepts my feelings and reactions and I can therefore trust God enough to express them honestly. In the imaginative encounter with Scripture I am invited to allow the full effects of the gospel mystery to penetrate my whole life and action so that I may be a more effective follower of Christ.

1. See *The Spiritual Exercises of St Ignatius*, trans. Louis J. Puhl, (Chicago 1951), nos 316–17 – cited subsequently as Exx.

2. See for example Matthias Neuman, 'Contemporary Spirituality of the Monastic *Lectio*', in *Review for Religious* (1977), pp. 97–100.

3. The method for gospel contemplation is described in a number of recent books. See, for example, John Veltri, *Orientations*, vol. 1 (Guelph, Ontario, 1979), pp. 25–7; Anthony de Mello, *Sadhana, a Way to God* (Gujarat/St Louis 1978), pp. 73ff; Christopher Bryant, *The River Within* (London 1980), pp. 85–8; Morton Kelsey, *Transcend* (New York 1981), pp. 101–10.

4. John Veltri, op. cit.

5. St Ignatius's brief description of the method is to be found in the second contemplation of the Second Week of the Exercises, Exx. 110–17.

6. For the origins of Ignatius's gospel contemplation, see for example Joseph de Guibert, *The Jesuits: Their Spiritual Doctrine and Practice* (St Louis 1972), ch. 4 *passim*, or James Walsh, 'Application of the Senses', in *The Way Supplement* 27 (Spring 1976), pp. 59–68. For a more detailed history of this method of prayer see Linda Spear, 'Prayer with Images', in *The Way* (July 1973), pp. 236–44.

7. Joseph Whelan, 'Contemplating Christ', in *The Way* (July 1970), p. 194.

8. For a general introduction to the relationship between Jung's understanding of imagiantion and Christian prayer see Christopher Bryant, *Jung and the Christian Way* (London 1983), and Morton Kelsey, *The Other Side of Silence* (New York 1976).

9. See for example, David Stanley, 'Revitalising our prayer through the Gospels' in *The Way Supplement* 19 (Summer 1973), pp. 3–12, and the subsequent discussion in a pamphlet of the same name which appeared in the series *Program to Adapt the Spiritual Exercises* (Jersey City 1973). Also Margot Donovan, 'Contemplating Christ Risen' in *The Way Supplement* 46 (Spring 1983), pp. 78–96.

10. See for example John Wickham, 'Ignatian Contemplation Today' in *The Way Supplement* 34 (Autumn 1978), pp. 35–44.